In 2012 will be:

Tryon - '98, 18 Sept. — 14

Tom
Tilly — 01, 18th May — Tryon's - 10

Katie - 02, 5th March - 10

Pippie - 05, May - 7

Roena - Sept 21 - 57

Peter - Feb. 22 - 64

Sam - March 6th - 55   married Nov. 26th
                                              2004
Barbara - Nov. 3rd - 59

Marty - May 14th - 54

Simon - Dec. 15th - 53

Celia - Dec. 2nd - 43

Richard - Feb. 13th, 1916 - 96

Me - Aug 13 - 1928 - 84

Kahlia (Sam's) July 17th - 24

We were married on May 16th - 1954
                                      62 years.
Jimmy - March 25 - '92 - Died
                    July 27th 2009

Richard died Sept. 16th - 1991, 75 yrs.
I will have been a Widow for 21 years in
                    Sept. 2012

TOTTERING-BY-GENTLY®

THE TOTTERINGS' DIARY 2012

BY JUPITER!
LONDON HOSTS OLYMPICS!
2012
TOTTERING
-BY-
GENTLY
KINGS ROAD
TO
STRATFORD

ANNIE TEMPEST

FRANCES LINCOLN LIMITED
PUBLISHERS

Frances Lincoln Limited
4 Torriano Mews
Torriano Avenue
London NW5 2RZ
www.franceslincoln.com

The Totterings' Desk Diary 2012
Text copyright © Annie Tempest 2011
Illustrations copyright © Annie Tempest 2011

Illustrations archived and compiled by
Raymond O'Shea

Every effort is made to ensure dates are correct at the time of going to press but the Publisher cannot accept liability for any errors or changes.

A catalogue record for this book is available from the British Library.

ISBN 978-0-7112-3193-1

Printed in China
Bound for North Pimmshire

9 8 7 6 5 4 3 2 1

Also available from Frances Lincoln at www.franceslincoln.com
Out and About with the Totterings
Drinks with the Totterings
The Tottering-by-Gently Annual
In the Garden with the Totterings
The Totterings' Pocket Diary 2012

To see a full range of Tottering-by-Gently licensed product visit The Tottering Drawing Room at The O'Shea Gallery, No. 4, St James's Street, London SW1A 1EF (Telephone +44 (0)207 930 5880) or visit the website at: www.tottering.com

CALENDAR 2012

JANUARY	FEBRUARY	MARCH	APRIL	MAY	JUNE
M T W T F S S	M T W T F S S	M T W T F S S	M T W T F S S	M T W T F S S	M T W T F S S
1	1 2 3 4 5	1 2 3 4	1	1 2 3 4 5 6	1 2 3
2 3 4 5 6 7 8	6 7 8 9 10 11 12	5 6 7 8 9 10 11	2 3 4 5 6 7 8	7 8 9 10 11 12 13	4 5 6 7 8 9 10
9 10 11 12 13 14 15	13 14 15 16 17 18 19	12 13 14 15 16 17 18	9 10 11 12 13 14 15	14 15 16 17 18 19 20	11 12 13 14 15 16 17
16 17 18 19 20 21 22	20 21 22 23 24 25 26	19 20 21 22 23 24 25	16 17 18 19 20 21 22	21 22 23 24 25 26 27	18 19 20 21 22 23 24
23 24 25 26 27 28 29	27 28 29	26 27 28 29 30 31	23 24 25 26 27 28 29	28 29 30 31	25 26 27 28 29 30
30 31			30		

JULY	AUGUST	SEPTEMBER	OCTOBER	NOVEMBER	DECEMBER
M T W T F S S	M T W T F S S	M T W T F S S	M T W T F S S	M T W T F S S	M T W T F S S
1	1 2 3 4 5	1 2	1 2 3 4 5 6 7	1 2 3 4	1 2
2 3 4 5 6 7 8	6 7 8 9 10 11 12	3 4 5 6 7 8 9	8 9 10 11 12 13 14	5 6 7 8 9 10 11	3 4 5 6 7 8 9
9 10 11 12 13 14 15	13 14 15 16 17 18 19	10 11 12 13 14 15 16	15 16 17 18 19 20 21	12 13 14 15 16 17 18	10 11 12 13 14 15 16
16 17 18 19 20 21 22	20 21 22 23 24 25 26	17 18 19 20 21 22 23	22 23 24 25 26 27 28	19 20 21 22 23 24 25	17 18 19 20 21 22 23
23 24 25 26 27 28 29	27 28 29 30 31	24 25 26 27 28 29 30	29 30 31	26 27 28 29 30	24 25 26 27 28 29 30
30 31					31

CALENDAR 2013

JANUARY	FEBRUARY	MARCH	APRIL	MAY	JUNE
M T W T F S S	M T W T F S S	M T W T F S S	M T W T F S S	M T W T F S S	M T W T F S S
1 2 3 4 5 6	1 2 3	1 2 3	1 2 3 4 5 6 7	1 2 3 4 5	1 2
7 8 9 10 11 12 13	4 5 6 7 8 9 10	4 5 6 7 8 9 10	8 9 10 11 12 13 14	6 7 8 9 10 11 12	3 4 5 6 7 8 9
14 15 16 17 18 19 20	11 12 13 14 15 16 17	11 12 13 14 15 16 17	15 16 17 18 19 20 21	13 14 15 16 17 18 19	10 11 12 13 14 15 16
21 22 23 24 25 26 27	18 19 20 21 22 23 24	18 19 20 21 22 23 24	22 23 24 25 26 27 28	20 21 22 23 24 25 26	17 18 19 20 21 22 23
28 29 30 31	25 26 27 28	25 26 27 28 29 30 31	29 30	27 28 29 30 31	24 25 26 27 28 29 30

JULY	AUGUST	SEPTEMBER	OCTOBER	NOVEMBER	DECEMBER
M T W T F S S	M T W T F S S	M T W T F S S	M T W T F S S	M T W T F S S	M T W T F S S
1 2 3 4 5 6 7	1 2 3 4	1	1 2 3 4 5 6	1 2 3	1
8 9 10 11 12 13 14	5 6 7 8 9 10 11	2 3 4 5 6 7 8	7 8 9 10 11 12 13	4 5 6 7 8 9 10	2 3 4 5 6 7 8
15 16 17 18 19 20 21	12 13 14 15 16 17 18	9 10 11 12 13 14 15	14 15 16 17 18 19 20	11 12 13 14 15 16 17	9 10 11 12 13 14 15
22 23 24 25 26 27 28	19 20 21 22 23 24 25	16 17 18 19 20 21 22	21 22 23 24 25 26 27	18 19 20 21 22 23 24	16 17 18 19 20 21 22
29 30 31	26 27 28 29 30 31	23 24 25 26 27 28 29	28 29 30 31	25 26 27 28 29 30	23 24 25 26 27 28 29
		30			30 31

THE O'SHEA GALLERY

Raymond O'Shea of The O'Shea Gallery was originally one of London's leading antiquarian print and map dealers. Historically, antiquarian galleries sponsored and promoted contemporary artists who they felt complemented their recognized areas of specialization. It was in this tradition that O'Shea first contacted *Country Life* magazine to see if Annie Tempest would like to be represented and sponsored by his gallery. In 1995 Raymond was appointed agent for Annie Tempest's originals and publisher of her books. Raymond is responsible for creating an archive of all of Annie's cartoons.

In 2003, the antiquarian side of his business was put on hold and the St. James's Street premises were finally converted to The Tottering Drawing Room at The O'Shea Gallery. It is now the flagship of a worldwide operation that syndicates and licenses illustrated books, prints, stationery, champagne, jigsaws, greetings cards, ties and much more. It has even launched its own fashion range of tweeds and shooting accessories under the label Gently Ltd.

The Tottering Drawing Room at The O'Shea Gallery is a wonderful location which is now available for corporate events of 45–125 people and is regularly used for private dinner parties catering for up to 14 people. Adjacent to St. James's Palace, the gallery lies between two famous 18th century shops: Berry Bros. & Rudd, the wine merchants and Locks, the hatters. Accessed through French doors at the rear of the gallery lies Pickering Place – not only the smallest public square in Great Britain, with original gas lighting, but it was also where the last duel in England was fought. A plaque on the wall, erected by the Anglo-Texan Society, indicates that from 1842–45 a building here was occupied by the Legation from the Republic of Texas to the Court of St. James.

Raymond O'Shea and Annie Tempest are delighted to be able to extend Tottering fans a warm welcome in the heart of historic St. James's where all the original Tottering watercolours can be seen along side a full product and print range.

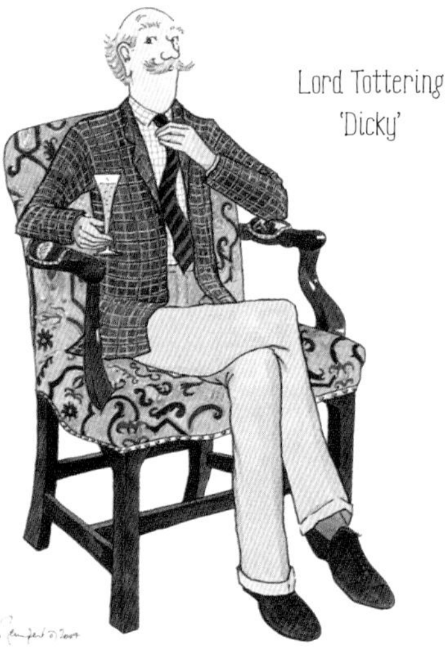
Lord Tottering
'Dicky'

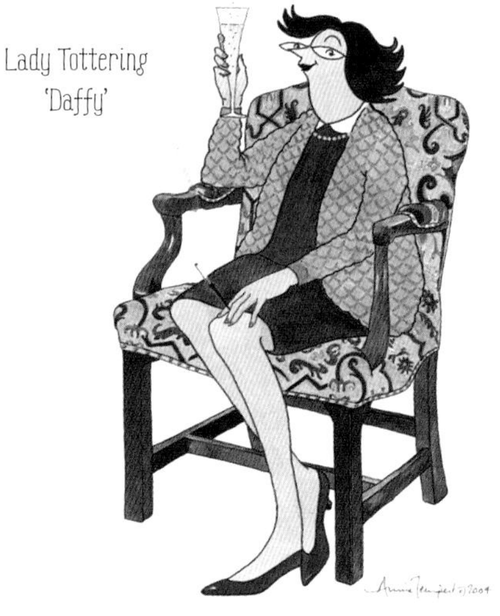
Lady Tottering
'Daffy'

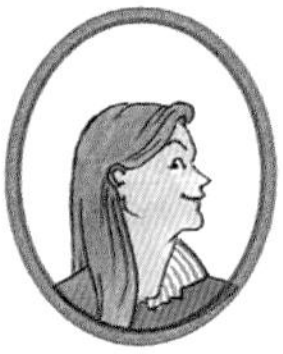
Serena

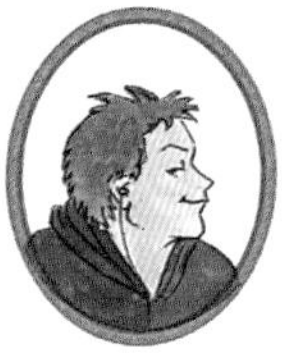
Freddy

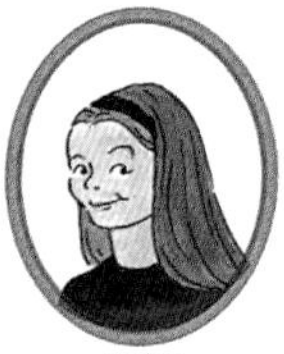
Daisy

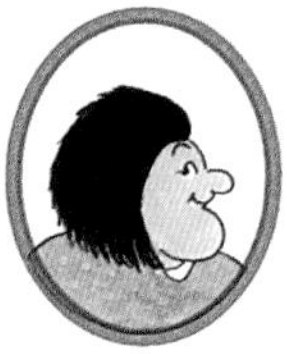
Gladys Shagpile

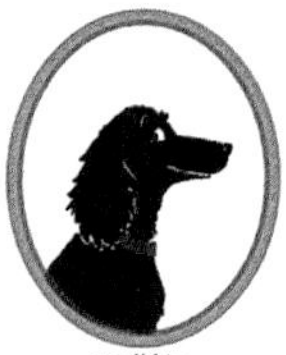
Scribble

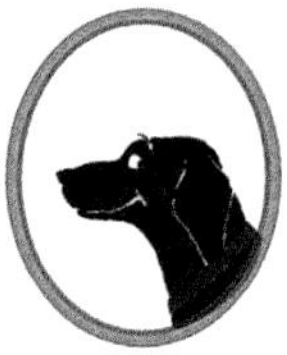
Slobber

TOTTERING-BY-GENTLY ®
ANNIE TEMPEST

Annie Tempest is one of the top cartoonists working in the UK. This was recognized in 2009 with the Cartoon Art Trust awarding her the Pont Prize for the portrayal of the British Character. Annie's cartoon career began in 1985 with the success of her first book, *How Green Are Your Wellies?* This led to a regular cartoon, 'Westenders' in the *Daily Express*. Soon after, she joined the *Daily Mail* with 'The Yuppies' cartoon strip which ran for more than seven years and for which, in 1989, she was awarded 'Strip Cartoonist of the Year'. Since 1993 Annie Tempest has been charting the life of Daffy and Dicky Tottering in Tottering-by-Gently – the phenomenally successful weekly strip cartoon in *Country Life*.

Daffy Tottering is a woman of a certain age who has been taken into the hearts of people all over the world. She reflects the problems facing women in their everyday life and is completely at one with herself, while reflecting on the intergenerational tensions and the differing perspectives of men and women, as well as dieting, ageing, gardening, fashion, food, field sports, convention and much more.

Daffy and her husband Dicky live in the fading grandeur of Tottering Hall, their stately home in the fictional county of North Pimmshire, with their extended family: son and heir Hon Jon,daughter Serena, and grandchildren, Freddy and Daisy. The daily, Mrs Shagpile, and love of Dicky's life, Slobber, his black Labrador, and the latest addition to the family, Scribble, Daisy's working Cocker Spaniel, also make regular appearances.

Annie Tempest was born in Zambia in 1959. She has a huge international following and has had eighteen one-woman shows, from Mexico to Mayfair. Her work is now syndicated from New York to Dubai.

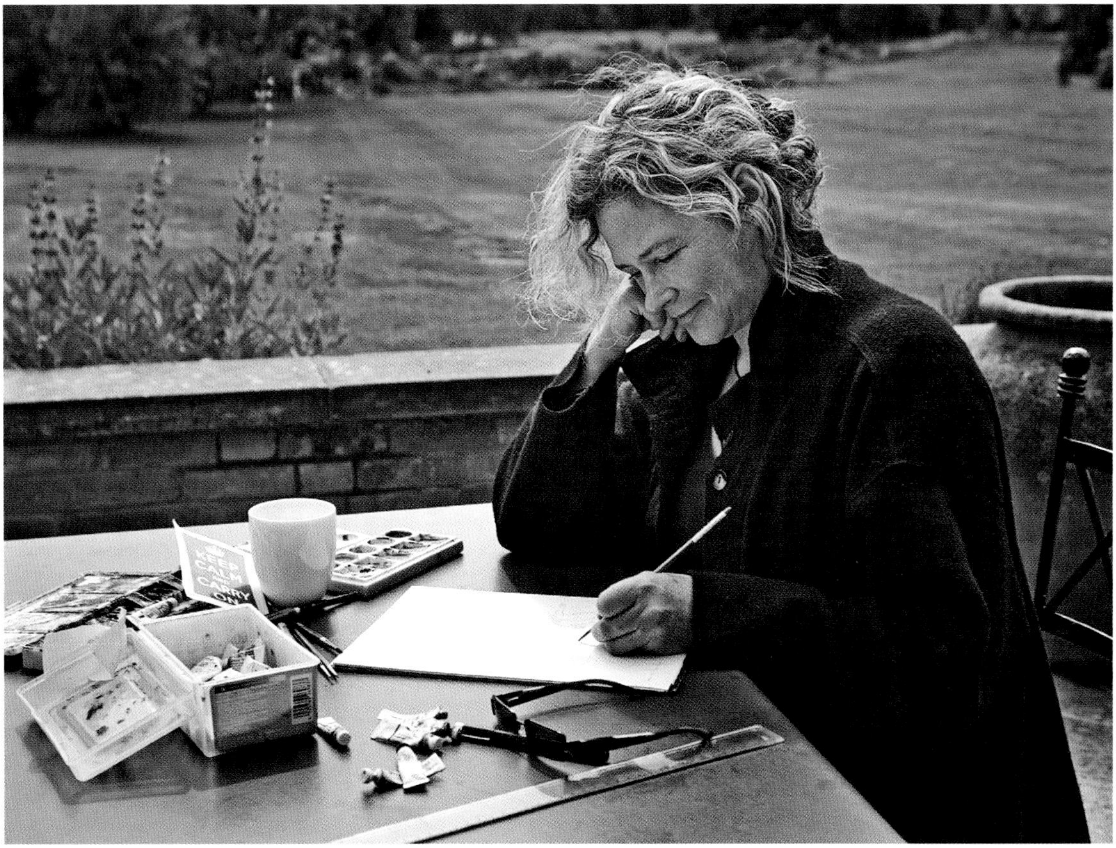

2010 © Garlinda Birkbeck

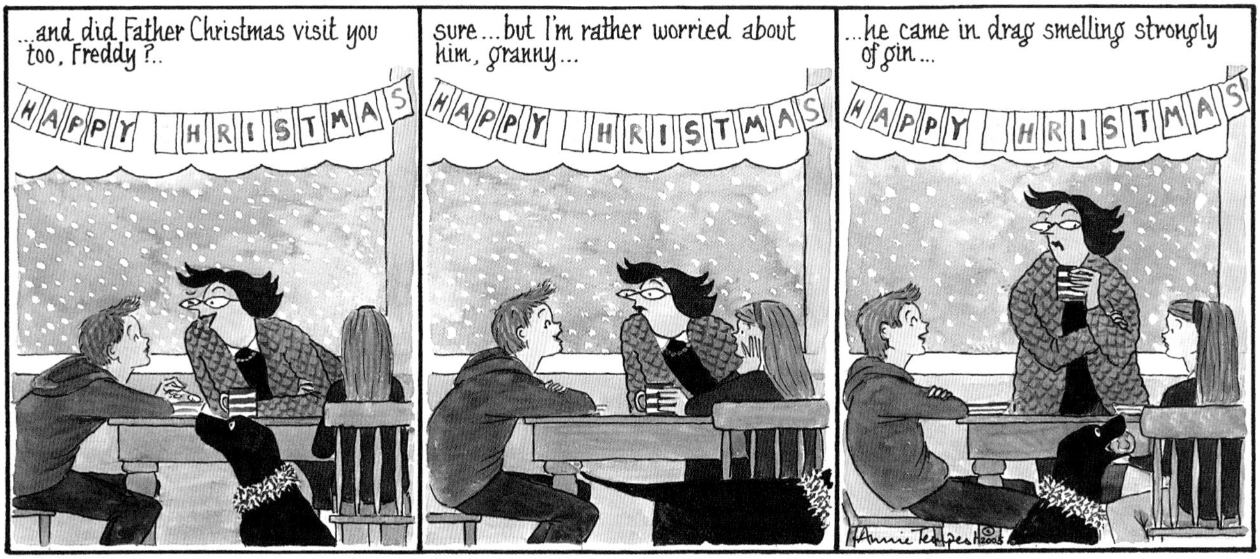
...and did Father Christmas visit you too, Freddy?..
HAPPY HRISTMAS
sure... but I'm rather worried about him, granny...
HAPPY HRISTMAS
...he came in drag smelling strongly of gin...
HAPPY HRISTMAS
Annie Tempest ©2005

DECEMBER - JANUARY

26 Monday

Boxing Day (St Stephen's Day)
Holiday, UK, Republic of Ireland, USA, Canada, Australia and New Zealand

27 Tuesday

Holiday, UK, Australia and New Zealand

28 Wednesday

29 Thursday

Cracked my Rib

30 Friday

31 Saturday

New Year's Eve

1 Sunday

First Quarter
New Year's Day
Holiday, Republic of Ireland

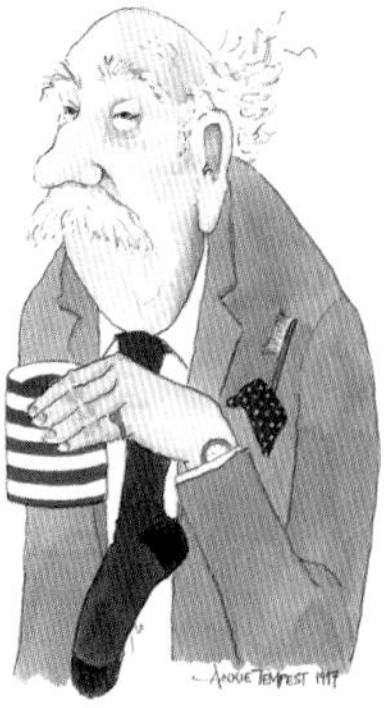

JANUARY

2 Monday — Holiday, UK, USA, Canada, Australia and New Zealand

3 Tuesday — Holiday, Scotland and New Zealand

4 Wednesday

Claremont - MRI - 12.20pm, Dr. Moore.

Phone call to say Money from investments would be in my account this afternoon.

5 Thursday

6 Friday — Epiphany

Beeley - The Stables - 12.30

Snow drops right out under the Laburnum tree

7 Saturday

8 Sunday

Mat shot 1 Rat

Right - I've given up smoking so what can I usefully do instead of lighting up...

...a challenging game of hat on the hoover...

Annie Tempest © 1999

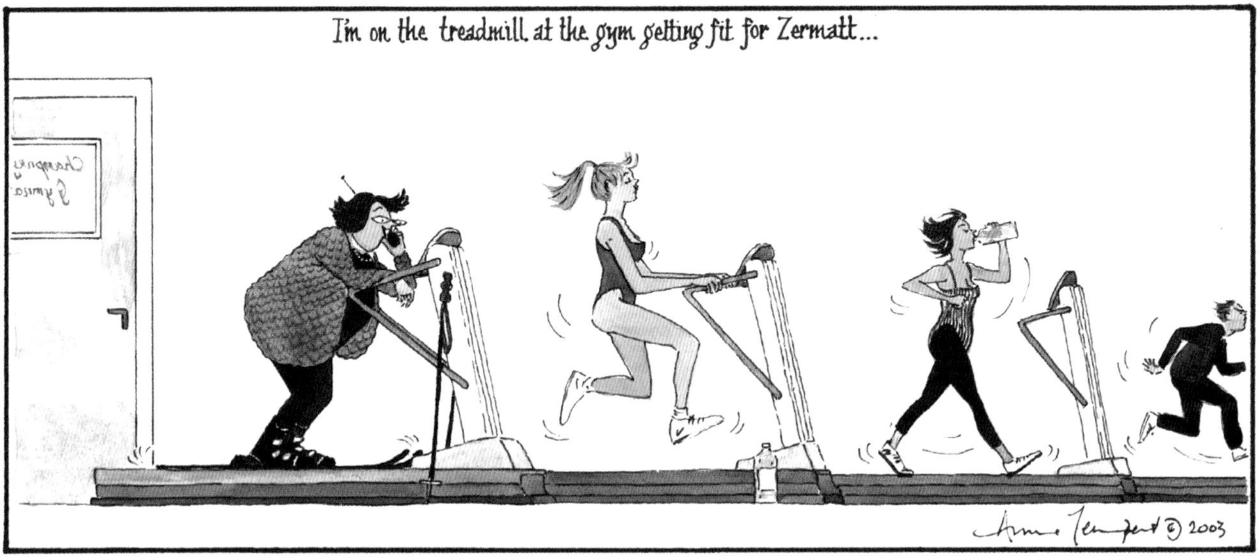
Anne Tempest © 2003

I'm on the treadmill at the gym getting fit for Zermatt...

9 Monday

10 Tuesday
collect Pills from Vet. The Gang,
The Gnowll - 12.30. Lovely weather

11 Wednesday

Rat man came - lo Boxes, poo. Rats.

12 Thursday

13 Friday
The Devonshire - Pilsley 12.30
am to Scotland.

Barlow: Barlow Lees and New

14 Saturday

15 Sunday
New Haven - cancelled, bad frost
unch at Royal Oak - Annette

JANUARY

16 Monday Sam home

Last Quarter
Holiday, USA (Martin Luther King's Birthday)

17 Tuesday 11am Peter Nolan and Dominic Stanniforth – 1 hour?

18 Wednesday

19 Thursday Luncheon Club – Kath Birkinshaw.

20 Friday Over Haddon

21 Saturday Barlow: Millthorpe/Kennels

22 Sunday

THE LABRADOR CHARACTER : Always at his master's heel...

Annie Tempest © 2005

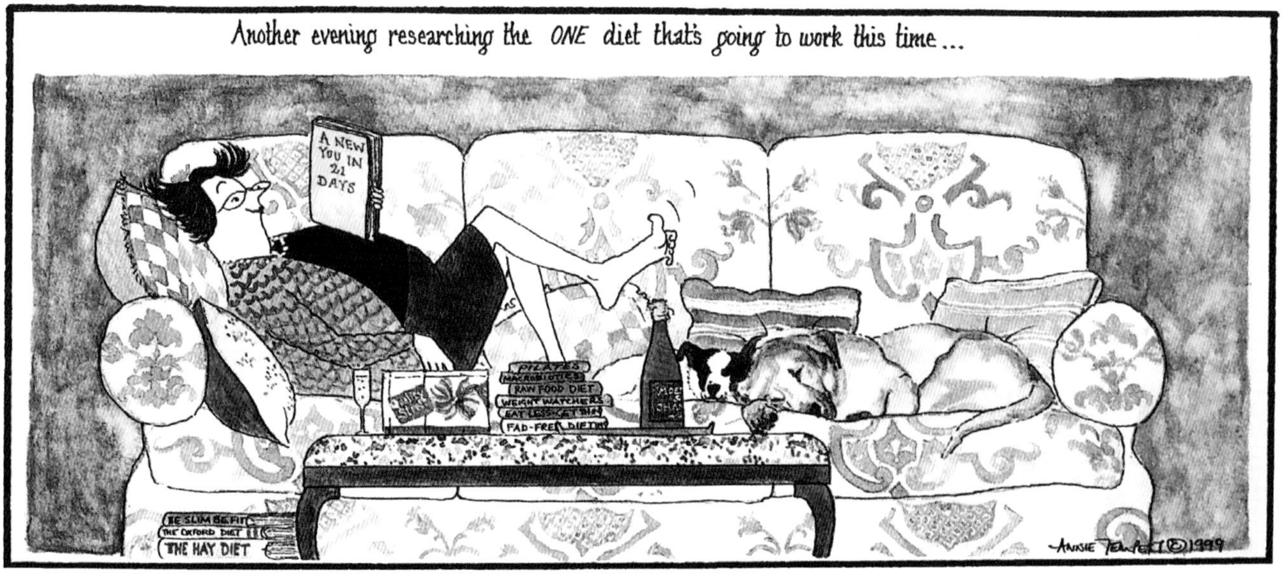
A NEW YOU IN 21 DAYS
PILATES
MACROBIOTICS
RAW FOOD DIET
WEIGHT WATCHERS
THE OXFORD DIET
THE HAY DIET

Another evening researching the *ONE* diet that's going to work this time...

JANUARY

23 Monday Stannah Stair Lift? Johnathan — *New Moon* Chinese New Year
9-12am - will phone

24 Tuesday
Mr. Porter - 2pm, Bakewell.

25 Wednesday

Ring Johnathan after 7pm

26 Thursday — Holiday, Australia (Australia Day)

27 Friday The Crispin - 12.30

Chris Bingham - Plumber, 4-5pm.

28 Saturday Barlow: Wilday Green

29 Sunday

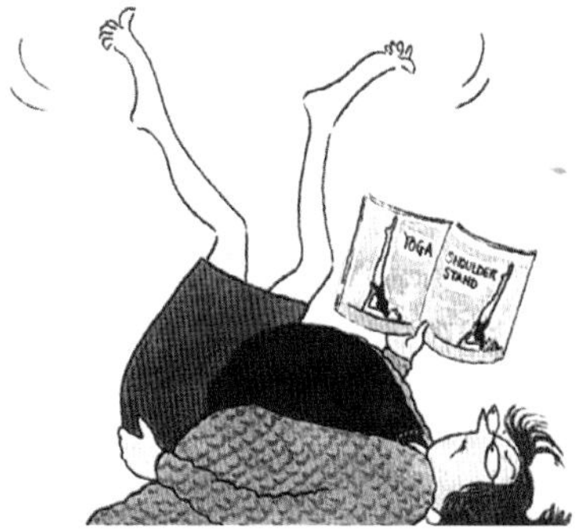
YOGA
SHOULDER STAND

JANUARY - FEBRUARY

30 Monday

31 Tuesday *First Quarter*

11am 33 Devonshire Road, Anne
Take Lap Top.

1 Wednesday

2 Thursday

3 Friday The Rutland — 12.30

4 Saturday

5 Sunday

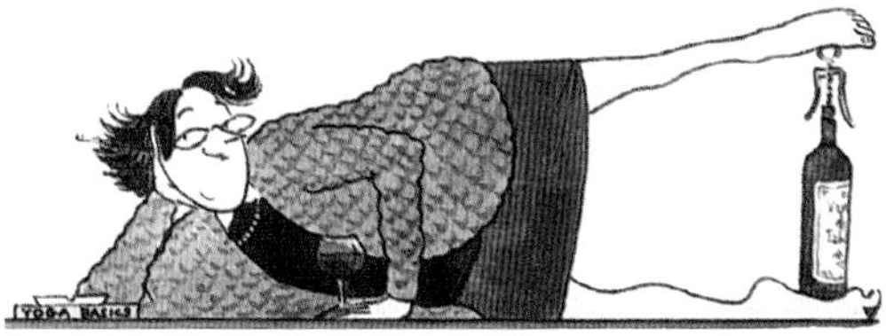

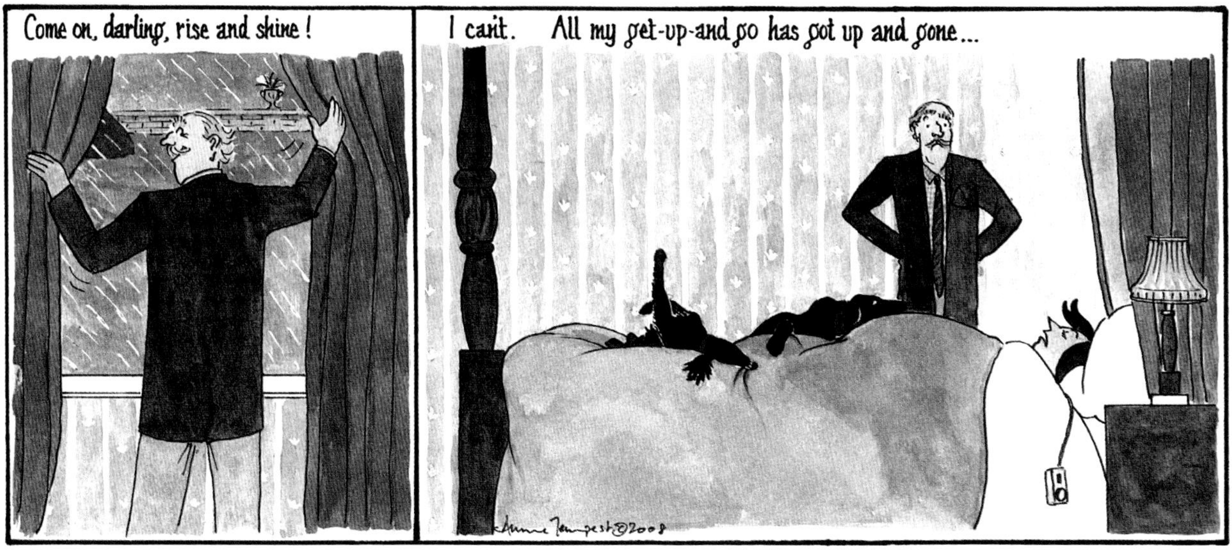
Come on, darling, rise and shine!
I can't. All my get-up-and go has got up and gone...
Annie Tempest©2008

Dicky Tottering was quite put out in White's last week...

an old chum went up to him after dinner and said...

"I say, old chap - aren't we both dead?..."

FEBRUARY

6 Monday   Vet - 10.50

Accession of Queen Elizabeth II (Diamond Jubilee)
Holiday, New Zealand (Waitangi Day)

7 Tuesday   The Gang - The Chequers - 12.30   *Full Moon*
Jo. 2.30 — To Lima

8 Wednesday

9 Thursday   Home from Lima

10 Friday

11 Saturday

12 Sunday

FEBRUARY

13 Monday Dentist - 11am

✳

RICHARD - 96

14 Tuesday

Last Quarter
St Valentine's Day

15 Wednesday

16 Thursday Mr. Getty - Claremont - 10.15

17 Friday Eyre Annual - 12.30

18 Saturday

19 Sunday Bloodhounds - Chatsworth House.

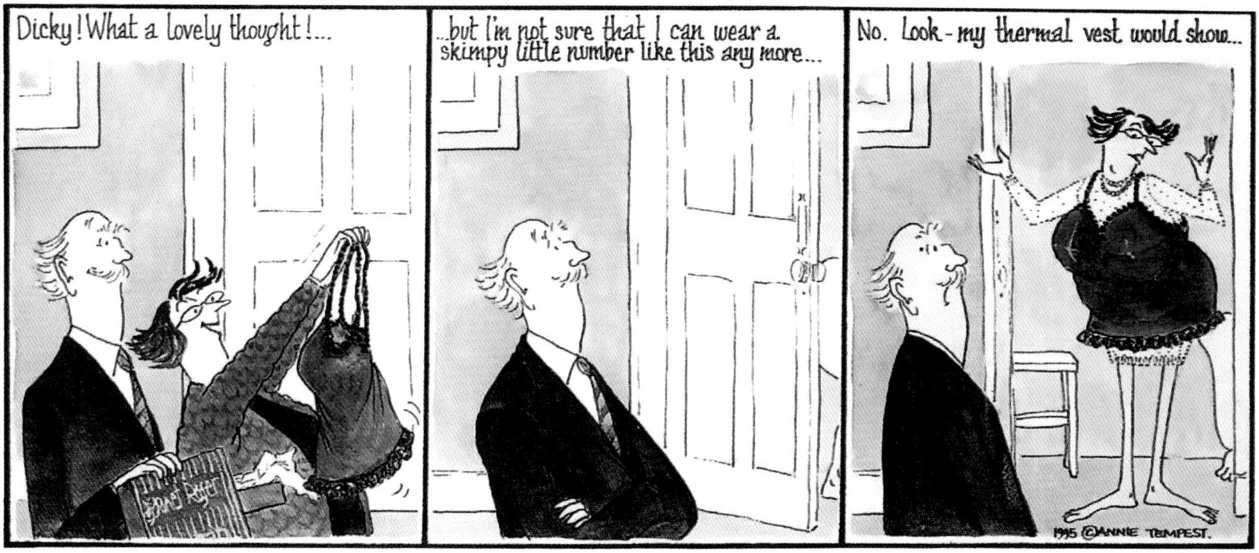
Dicky! What a lovely thought!...
...but I'm not sure that I can wear a skimpy little number like this any more...
No. Look - my thermal vest would show...
1995 ©ANNIE TEMPEST.

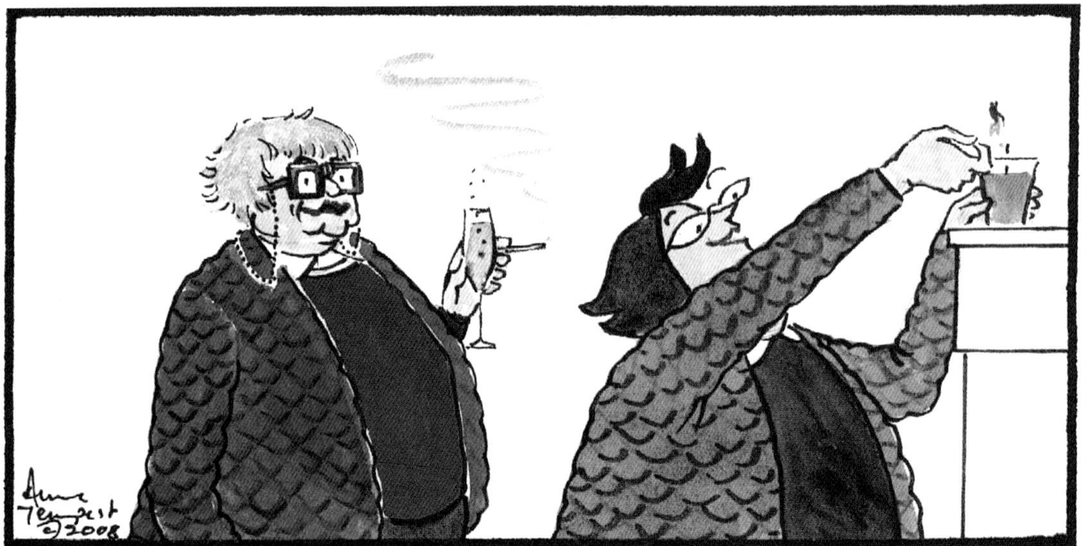
Anne Tempest ©2008

I love these scented candles Dicky gives me for Christmas -
So good for hiding the smell of dead mice under the floorboards..

FEBRUARY

20 Monday — Holiday, USA (Washington's Birthday)

2pm - Claremont - Ian B. Physio

21 Tuesday — *New Moon* — Shrove Tuesday

TREVOR * 89

22 Wednesday — Ash Wednesday

PETER - 64 *

23 Thursday

9.30 - Welsh Rechners

24 Friday

The Devonshire Arms - BEELEY - 12.30

25 Saturday

26 Sunday

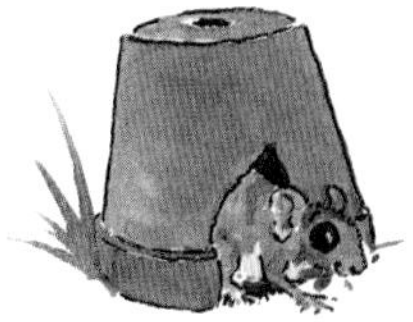

RING VET 8.30am to Cancel

27 Monday

Dentist - Hann 10.50am

The Vets - 4.30pm

Claremont 2.30

Baslow Hill closed

28 Tuesday Van for Ian - MOT (licence)

* Tilly put to sleep.

Roma and Peter to Wales

29 Wednesday

2.30 - Cockentown

1 Thursday Welsh Richness 9.30 ??

First Quarter
St David's Day

Baslow Hill open?

2 Friday

3 Saturday

4 Sunday Hoe Grange

Roma and Peter home?

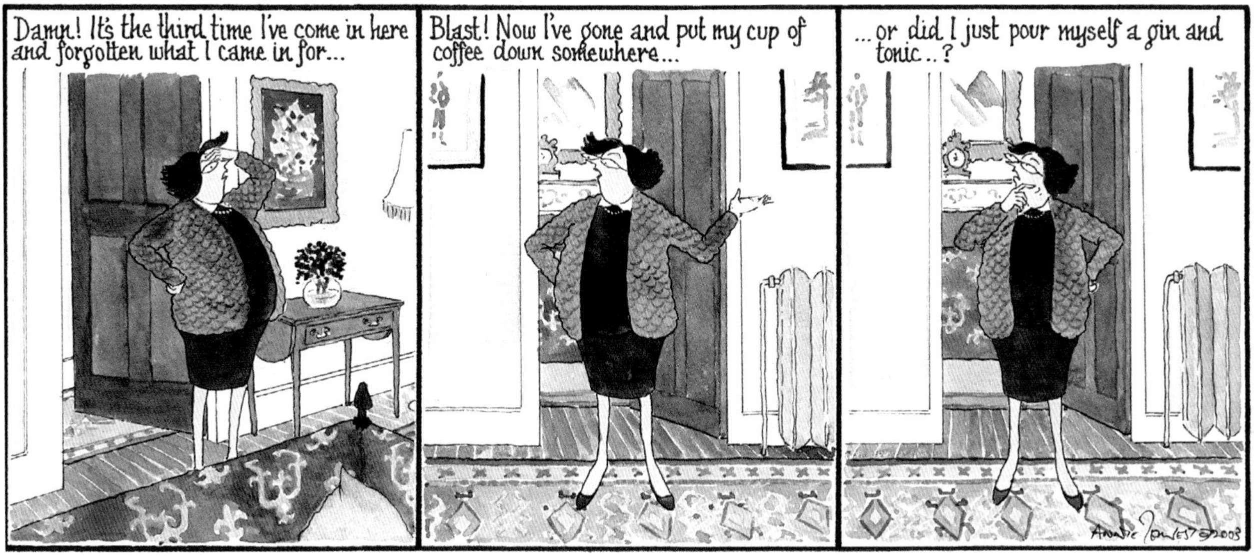
Damn! It's the third time I've come in here and forgotten what I came in for...
Blast! Now I've gone and put my cup of coffee down somewhere...
...or did I just pour myself a gin and tonic..?

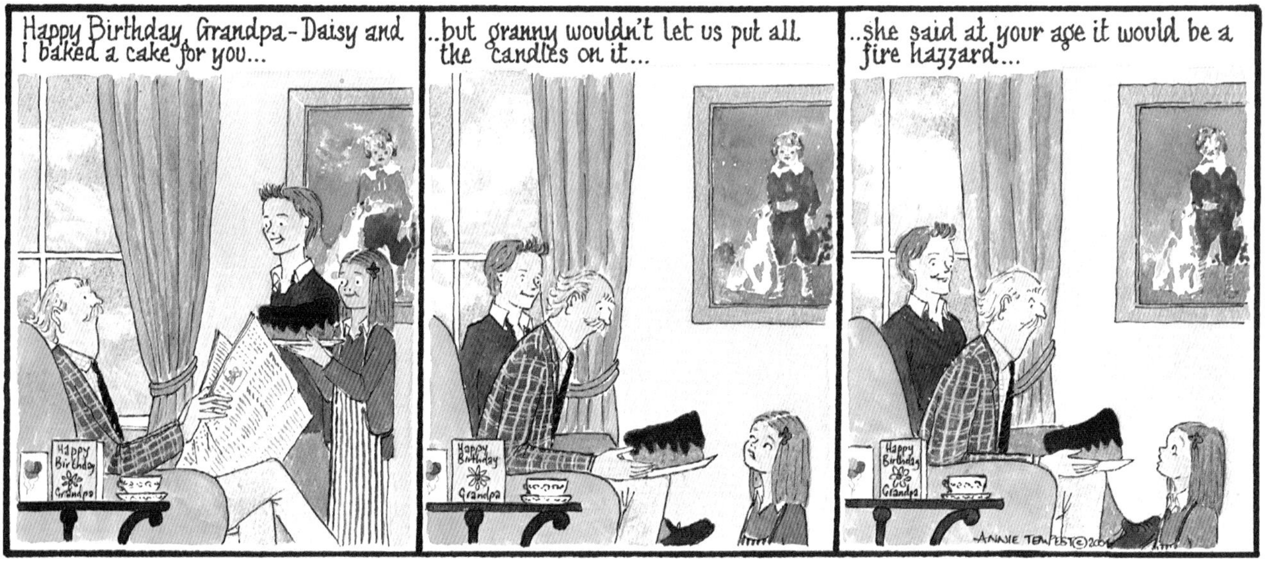
Happy Birthday, Grandpa - Daisy and I baked a cake for you...
Happy Birthday Grandpa
..but granny wouldn't let us put all the candles on it...
Happy Birthday Grandpa
..she said at your age it would be a fire hazzard...
Happy Birthday Grandpa
ANNIE TEMPEST

MARCH

WEEK 11

5 Monday

3.30 Physio - Claremont

6 Tuesday SAM - 55 *

Tom to Vet 11am

7 Wednesday

8 Thursday

Full Moon

9 Friday

Biffe - 12.30

10 Saturday

11 Sunday Sandbeck 10.45

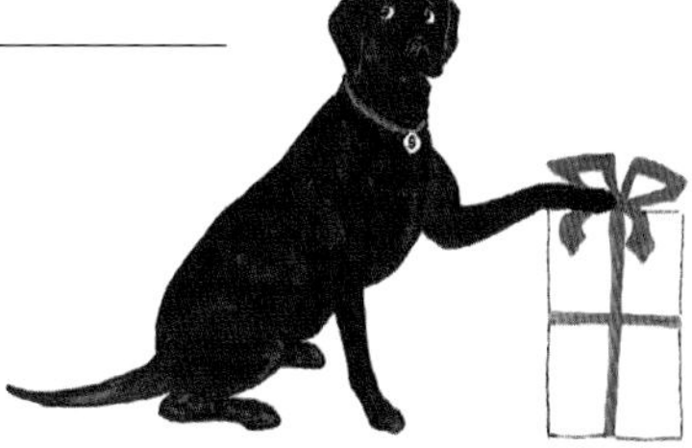

Maltby - Tickhill - Oldcotes

Dinnington

MARCH

WEEK 12

12 Monday — Commonwealth Day

Eye Place 3.15-30

13 Tuesday

Claremont - 3.30pm

14 Wednesday

15 Thursday — *Last Quarter*

Ladies luncheon - 1pm

16 Friday Riverside - Ashford - 12.30

17 Saturday Barlow around - last? — St Patrick's Day, Holiday, Republic of Ireland

18 Sunday Organ Ground? — Mother's Day, UK

Anyone here got any good news?
No?...
NEW SUICIDE BOMBING CAMPAIGN
TAXES UP!
ABDUCTION
Good. I wouldn't want anything to spoil a perfectly bloody day...

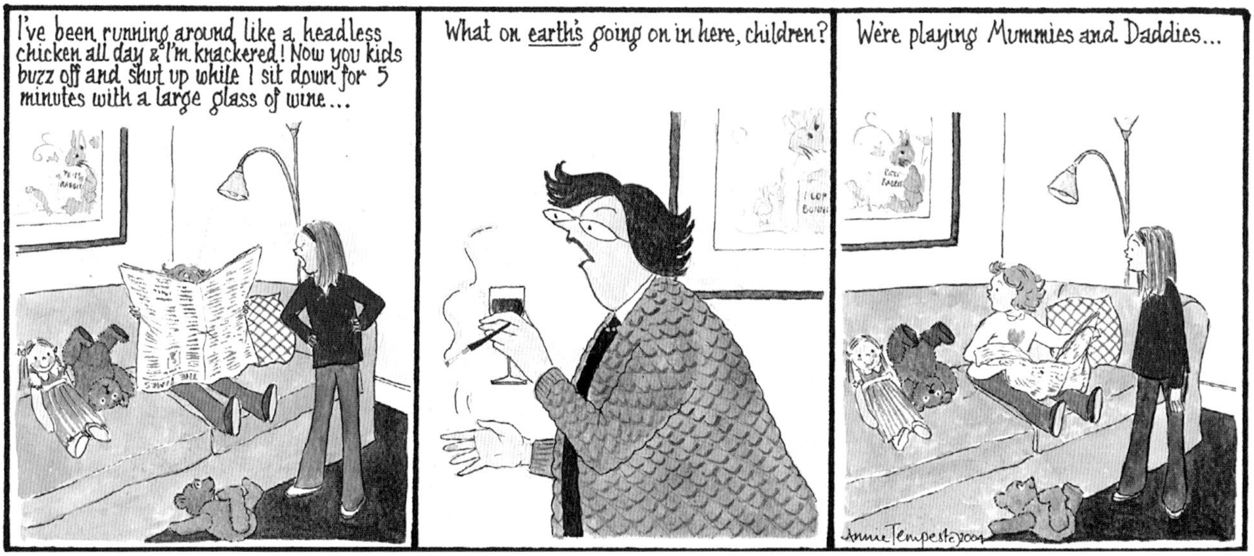
I've been running around like a headless chicken all day & I'm knackered! Now you kids buzz off and shut up while I sit down for 5 minutes with a large glass of wine...
What on earth's going on in here, children?
We're playing Mummies and Daddies...
Annie Tempest

MARCH

---

19 Monday — Holiday, Northern Ireland (St Patrick's Day)

---

20 Tuesday — Vernal Equinox (Spring begins)

The Gang - Toby Grill
Ecclesall. 12.30

---

21 Wednesday

---

22 Thursday — *New Moon*

Tinsley - Bloodhounds ? (1s 2 B 3)

---

23 Friday

Over Haddon

---

24 Saturday

---

25 Sunday — British Summer Time begins

JIMMY - 93 *

Worksop - Callow Carr Farm ?

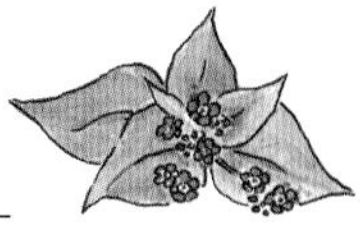

26 Monday

Physiotherapy - Claremont - 3.30

27 Tuesday

SUE ROUSE *

2pm - Dominic Stanniforth

28 Wednesday

6.30pm Simon & Celia Dim Sum

29 Thursday

30 Friday

First Quarter

Ashford - The Bull - 12.30

31 Saturday

1 Sunday

Palm Sunday

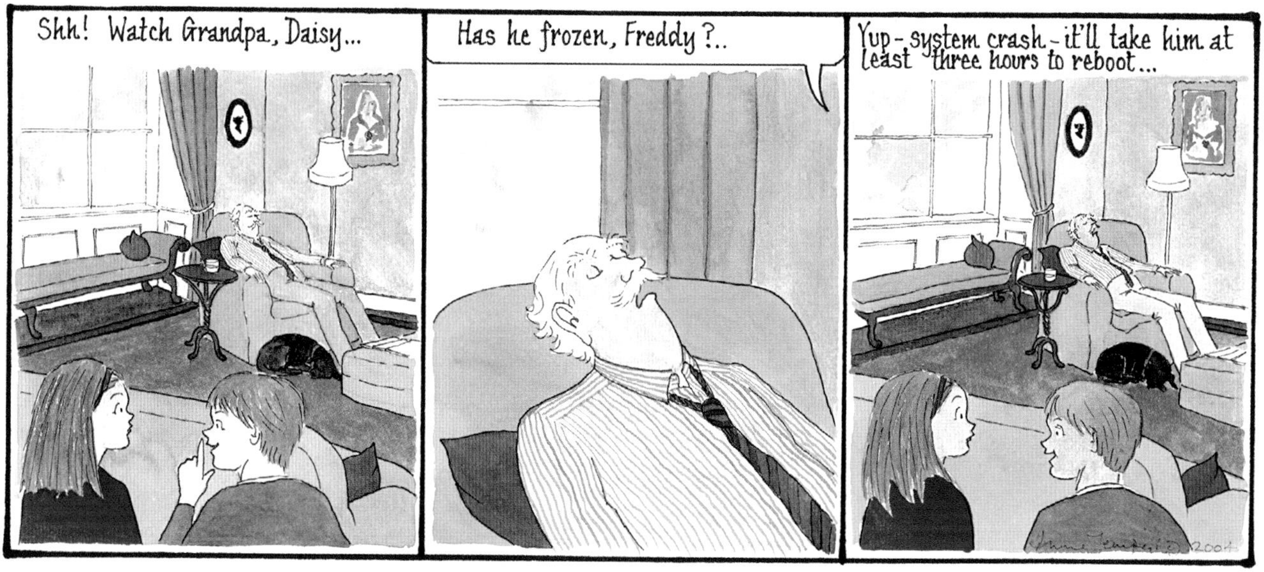
Shh! Watch Grandpa, Daisy...
Has he frozen, Freddy?..
Yup - system crash - it'll take him at least three hours to reboot...

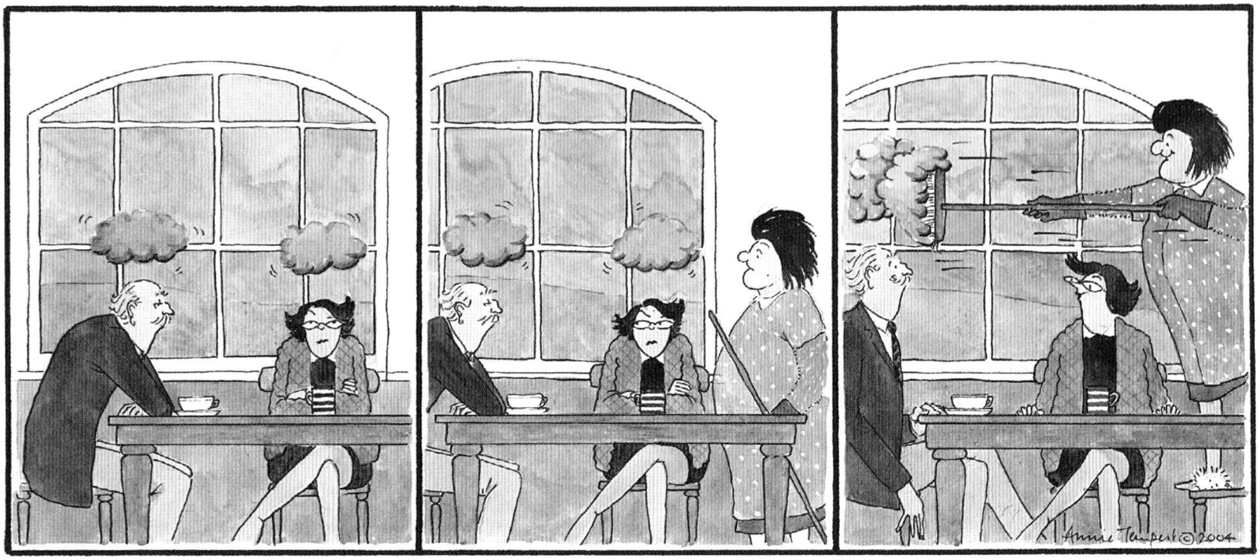
Annie Tempest © 2004

APRIL

2 Monday Felix Nolan to phone. – didn't

3 Tuesday So I phoned him!

~~Cockerton – 2.30~~

4 Wednesday phone Farmer's Garage ✓

5 Thursday — Maundy Thursday

6 Friday Fellinis – 12.30

Full Moon
Good Friday
Holiday, UK, Canada, Australia and New Zealand

7 Saturday Buy Eggs – and Pie?
lunch with Molly – Crispin

Holiday, Australia (Easter Saturday)
First Day of Passover (Pesach)

8 Sunday — Easter Sunday

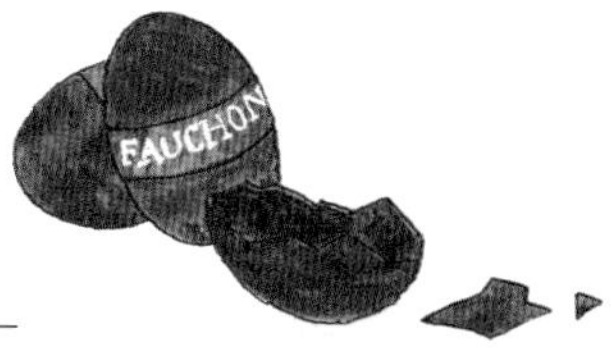
FAUCHON

APRIL

9 Monday No milk or papers

Easter Monday
Holiday, UK (exc. Scotland), Republic of Ireland
Australia and New Zealand

10 Tuesday Plumber - 9 am
Gang lunch - Owlerbar - 12.30
~~Physio: Claremont 2.30~~
Shop meeting - The Trout - 7.30 pm

11 Wednesday

Physio - Claremont - 4.30

12 Thursday

2.30 - Cockerton

13 Friday Milk?

The Devonshire - Pilsley - 12.30

Last Quarter

14 Saturday

15 Sunday

A really special Queen Anne walnut settee, is it? Well, it's not half as comfy as an old towel in a basket, if you ask me...

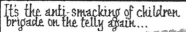

It's the anti-smacking of children brigade on the telly again....

I don't know. But I'd never raise my hand to our grandchildren.—would you, Dicky?

Certainly not—it would leave my groin unprotected....

16 Monday

12.30 - Annette's lunch

17 Tuesday

18 Wednesday

Pam - 12.45 Chalsfield
Sam ?

lunch
supper

19 Thursday

Ladies luncheon 1pm

lunch?
supper

20 Friday

Pam off: 9.20 Chest. ✱ 4 swallows
in Yard.
Eyre Ann d - 12.30
Tom - X Rays - 10 am Vet

21 Saturday

Pick up Annette, 12.30

New Moon
Birthday of Queen Elizabeth II

ROENA HEARD A CUCKOO. ✱

22 Sunday

Barlow Hunter Trials.

RING DENTIST, TO CANCEL.

23 Monday St George's Day

Diane here
Kate and Tegan to Vet. 11am

24 Tuesday

Diane here ~~Copen to lau-light~~
9am Plumber

25 Wednesday Holiday, Australia and New Zealand (Anzac Day)

Diane pre-wed.
2pm – Dentist – Wait

26 Thursday

27 Friday

The Rutland – 12.30

28 Saturday

Roena – 6pm to be collected by Simon

29 Sunday First Quarter

Roena ?

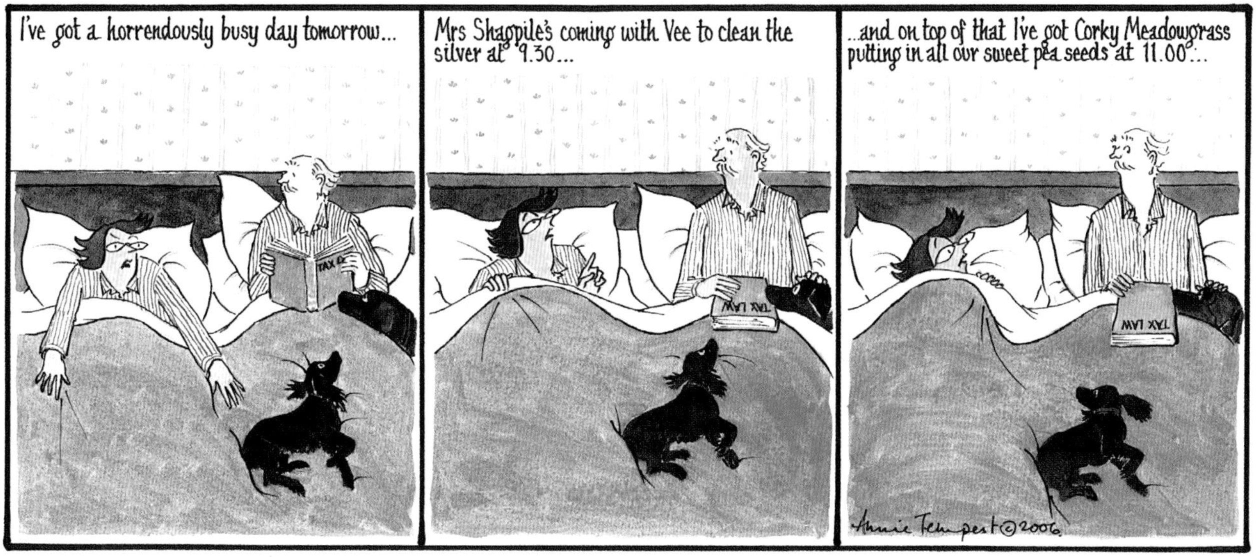
I've got a horrendously busy day tomorrow...
TAX
Mrs Shagpile's coming with Vee to clean the silver at 9.30...
TAX LAW
...and on top of that I've got Corky Meadowgrass putting in all our sweet pea seeds at 11.00...
TAX LAW
Annie Tempest © 2006

A drop more wine, Daffy?
No thanks, darling - I told you, I'm being good...
...I'm limiting myself to only one glass a night...
Annie Tempest © 2008

30 Monday Rosena home

Dentist — 11.10am

Barlow – Alison leaving – George + Drag on
7.30 onwards

1 Tuesday The Gang – The Peacock, Owler Bar,
12.30

2 Wednesday SUE HILYARD – 86? *

Nigel – 11am Cnass
Sam – back about 6pm Chesterfield.

3 Thursday Sam?

2.30 Cockertons

4 Friday

Rosena?

5 Saturday Rosena

6 Sunday Rosena?   *Full Moon*

MAY

---

7 Monday *ricona hour* Early Spring Bank Holiday, UK and Republic of Ireland

---

8 Tuesday

---

9 Wednesday

2.40 Dentist

J. Case - Plumber in eve with Kwik Sue

10 Thursday

---

11 Friday

The Stable - Beeley - 12.30

Cockerton - 3pm

---

12 Saturday *Last Quarter*

Sam to Wra

13 Sunday Mother's Day, USA, Canada, Australia and New Zealand

Sam will Wra - until eve

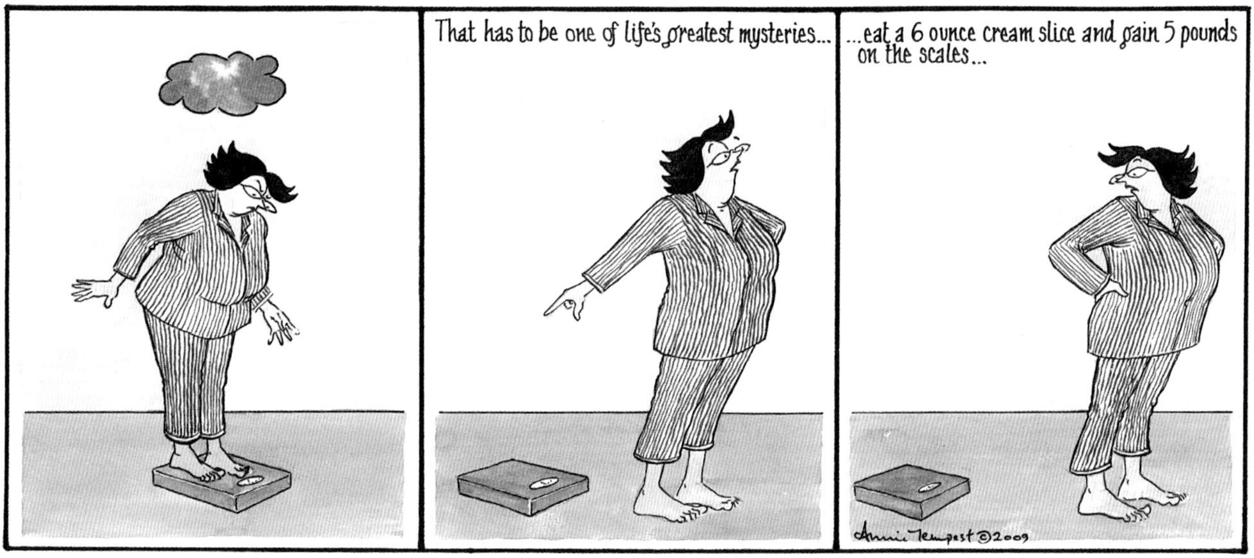
That has to be one of life's greatest mysteries...
...eat a 6 ounce cream slice and gain 5 pounds on the scales...
Annie Tempest ©2009

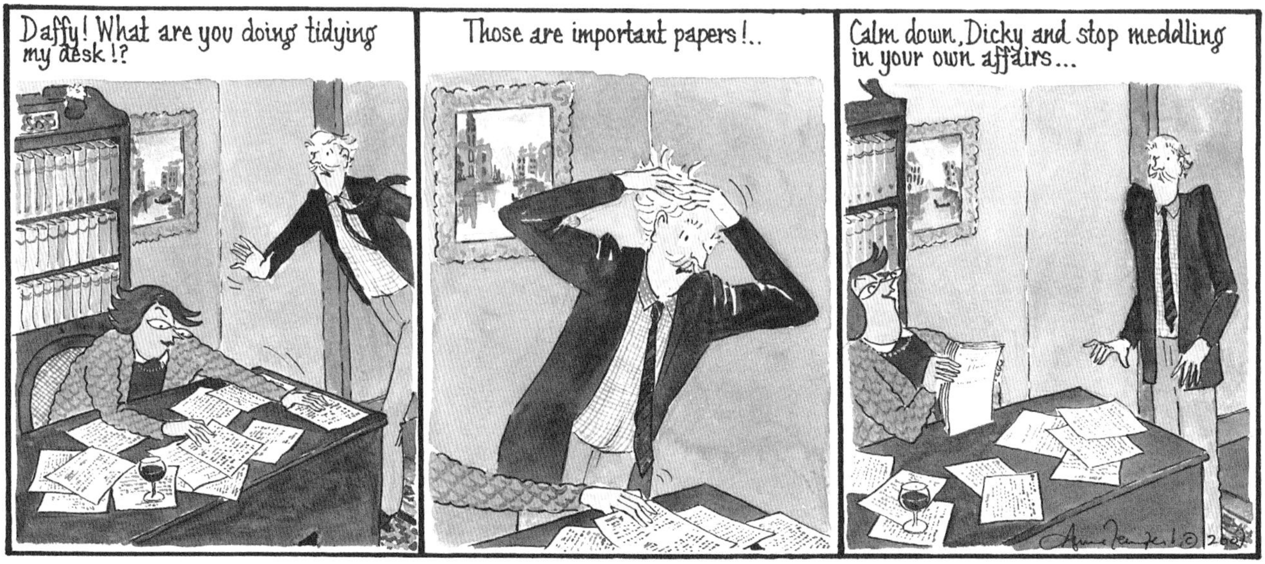
Daffy! What are you doing tidying my desk!?
Those are important papers!..
Calm down, Dicky and stop meddling in your own affairs...

MAY

14 Monday Sam home
11am Around Susanne Poole, Cockerton.

15 Tuesday Annette away / Sam off

16 Wednesday Celia home ... To Celia

17 Thursday Ascension Day
The Dentist — 11.40am
Celia home

18 Friday

19 Saturday

20 Sunday New Moon

21 Monday — Holiday, Canada (Victoria Day)

22 Tuesday

Annette home

23 Wednesday

24 Thursday

Wales enquiries to phone

25 Friday

Dentist - 10am

26 Saturday

Marty

27 Sunday — Whit Sunday (Pentecost)
Feast of Weeks (Shavuot)

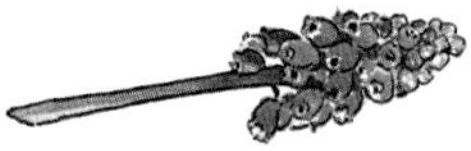

Miss Buffy Tip-Moth.

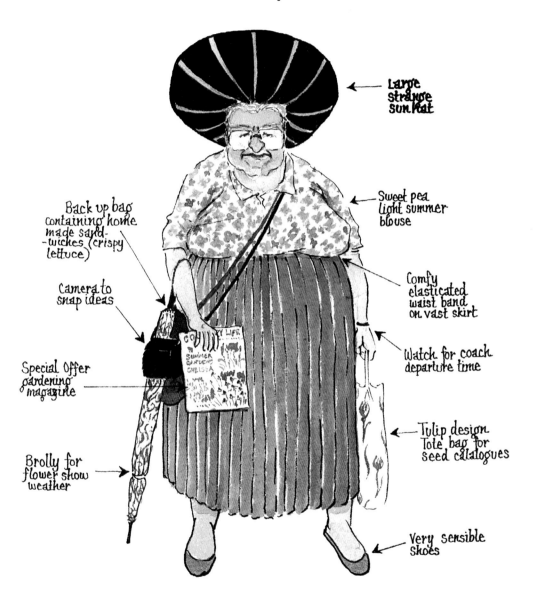

Large strange sun hat

Sweet pea light summer blouse

Comfy elasticated waist band on vast skirt

Watch for coach departure time

Tulip design Tote bag for seed catalogues

Very sensible shoes

Back up bag containing home made sand--wiches (crispy lettuce)

Camera to snap ideas

Special Offer gardening magazine

Brolly for flower show weather

COUNTRY LIFE
SUMMER GARDENS CHELSEA

FLOWER SHOW VISITOR
THE HARDY PERENNIAL

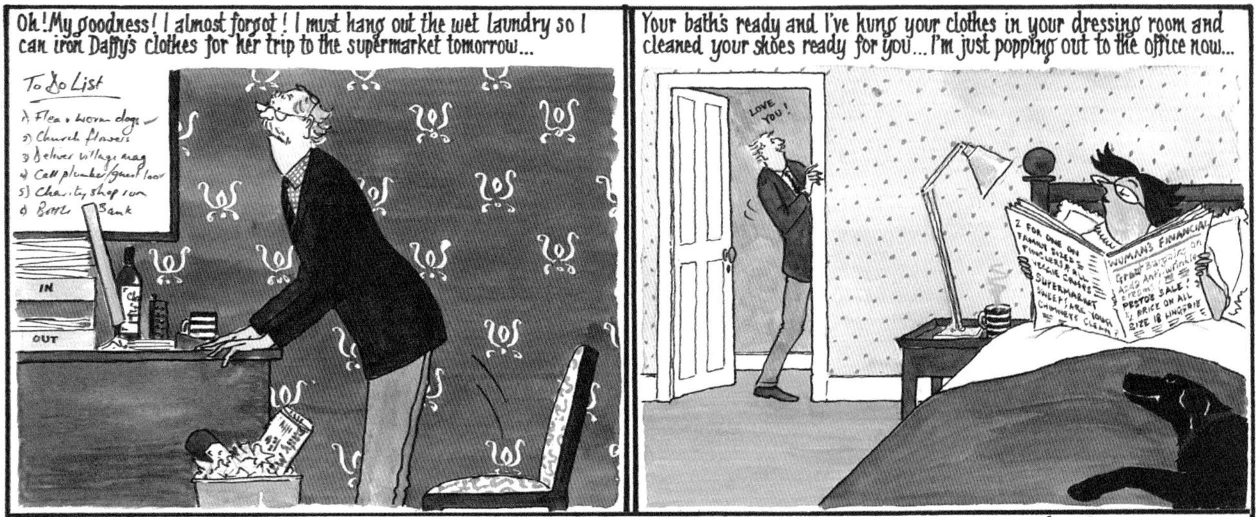
Oh! My goodness! I almost forgot! I must hang out the wet laundry so I can iron Daffy's clothes for her trip to the supermarket tomorrow...
To Do List
1) Flea & worm dogs
2) Church flowers
3) Deliver village mag
5) Charity shop run
IN
OUT
Your bath's ready and I've hung your clothes in your dressing room and cleaned your shoes ready for you... I'm just popping out to the office now...
LOVE YOU!
SUPERMARKET
PESTOS SALE!
SIZE 18 LINGERIE

NOT THE BRITISH CHARACTER...

MAY - JUNE

28 Monday

First Quarter
Holiday, USA (Memorial Day)

Mr. Getty - Claremont - 5.30pm

29 Tuesday

Rising Sun

30 Wednesday

31 Thursday

1 Friday

Annette to London

2 Saturday

Coronation Day

3 Sunday

Trinity Sunday

JUNE

4 Monday Bamford SDT lunch
Mrs M.E Simpson
Molly's 1pm - Heather Reeve's Do.

Full Moon
Spring Bank Holiday, UK
Holiday, Republic of Ireland
Holiday, New Zealand (The Queen's Birthday)

5 Tuesday

Holiday, UK (The Queen's Diamond Jubilee)

Annette home

6 Wednesday

7 Thursday

Corpus Christi

8 Friday

9 Saturday Barlow Show
Cancelled

The Queen's Official Birthday (subject to confirmation)

10 Sunday Barlow Show Cancelled

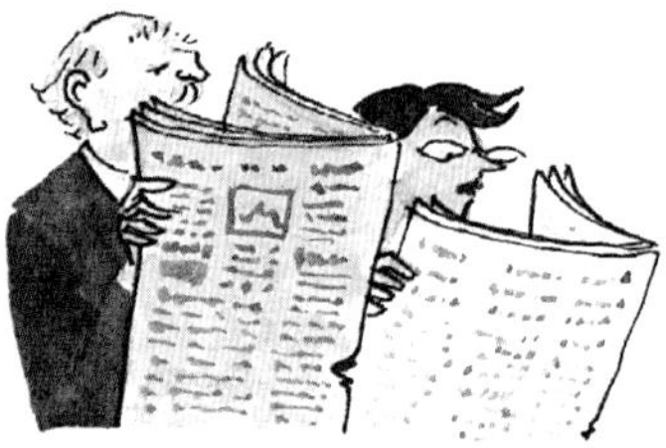

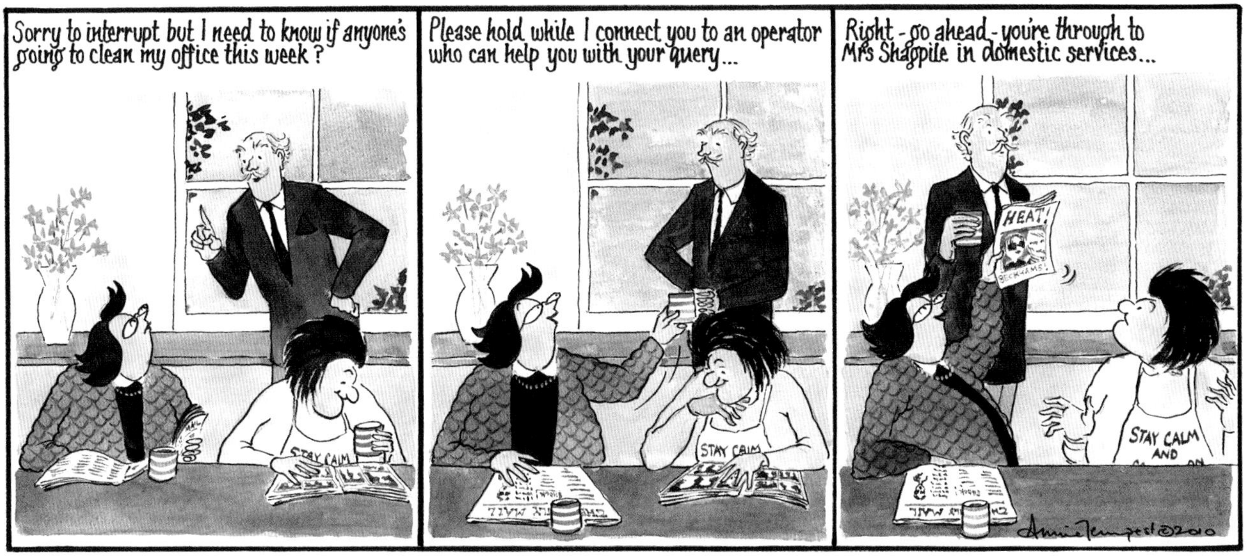
Sorry to interrupt but I need to know if anyone's going to clean my office this week?
STAY CALM
Please hold while I connect you to an operator who can help you with your query...
STAY CALM
Right - go ahead - you're through to Mrs Shagpile in domestic services...
HEAT!
BECKHAMS!
STAY CALM
AND
Annie Tempest ©2010

ANY PORT IN A STORM...

JUNE

11 Monday Bailey Johns - 8 am

Last Quarter

Holiday, Australia (The Queen's Birthday), subject to confirmation

12 Tuesday

13 Wednesday ~~[illegible]~~

14 Thursday Judy · Catenack - Chesterfield

15 Friday Monsal Head

Mat to Scotland for a week.

16 Saturday

Garden Party - Owl End - 2-6pm

17 Sunday Ring Annette A.M.

Father's Day, UK, Canada and USA

Garden Party - Owl End - 2-6pm

JUNE

18 Monday Wilf 8.30am onwards

19 Tuesday Wilf again - 8.30 am

New Moon

20 Wednesday Jo Salmon back away

Summer Solstice (Summer begins)

Boffin meeting at Gatel - 10am Coffee, cheese and biscuits

21 Thursday Burglar NO.

Ladies luncheon - 'Hats' 1pm Sit

22 Friday White Lion - Longstone, 12.30

23 Saturday - to Rome?

24 Sunday

Grandpa, why is the Land Rover always so muddy?

Because grandchildren won't do it for free any more...

...and employing someone to clean it can be the difference between profit and loss on an estate like this...

At our age we should be doing Sudoku puzzles or at the very least a daily dementia check...
...apparently, you start at 100 and subtract 7 as many times and as quickly as you can.
OK. Where's the calculator?..

25 Monday

26 Tuesday Home from Roena ?

27 Wednesday PAT DIED - 3am 2001 ✳ *First Quarter*
Shane

to 3

28 Thursday to Scrimson back.

29 Friday MARGRET KEEP - 83 ✳
to Kirkdale Hotel - Dee Haddon . 12.30

30 Saturday Scrimson ~ Colin away.

1 Sunday Canada Day, Canada

Barton Puppy Show - 3.30pm

JULY

2 Monday   Holiday, Canada (Canada Day)

3 Tuesday   *Full Moon*

4 Wednesday   Holiday, USA (Independence Day)

5 Thursday *Hairdresser – 2.15*

Lou Gatty Ring Card

6 Friday *Rowleys – 12.30*

7 Saturday *Mat ?*

8 Sunday *Mat ?*

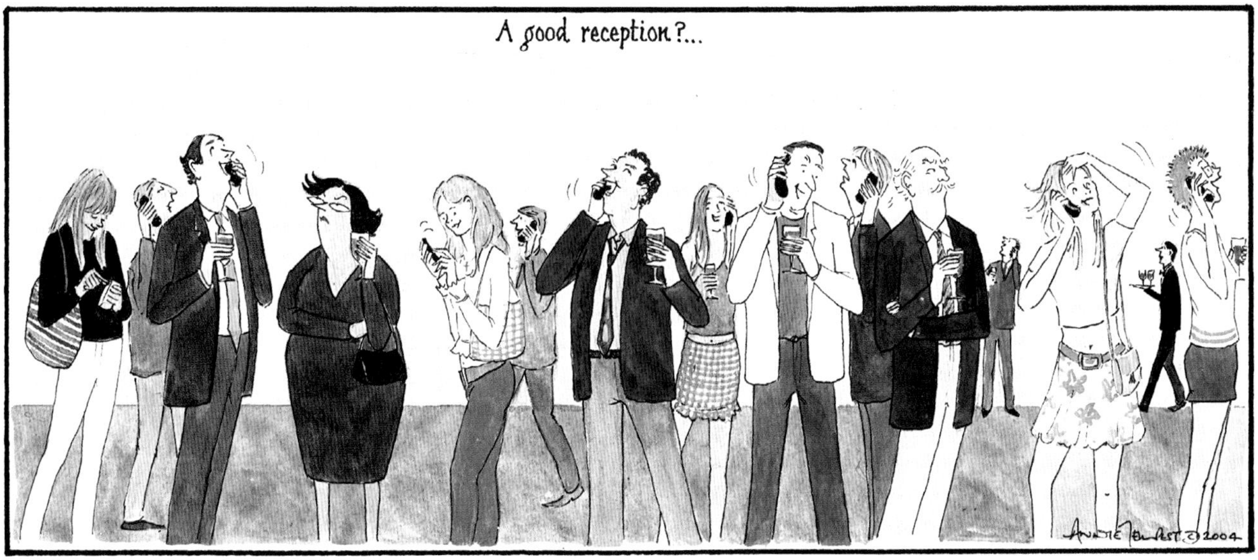
ANNIE TEMPEST © 2004
A good reception?...

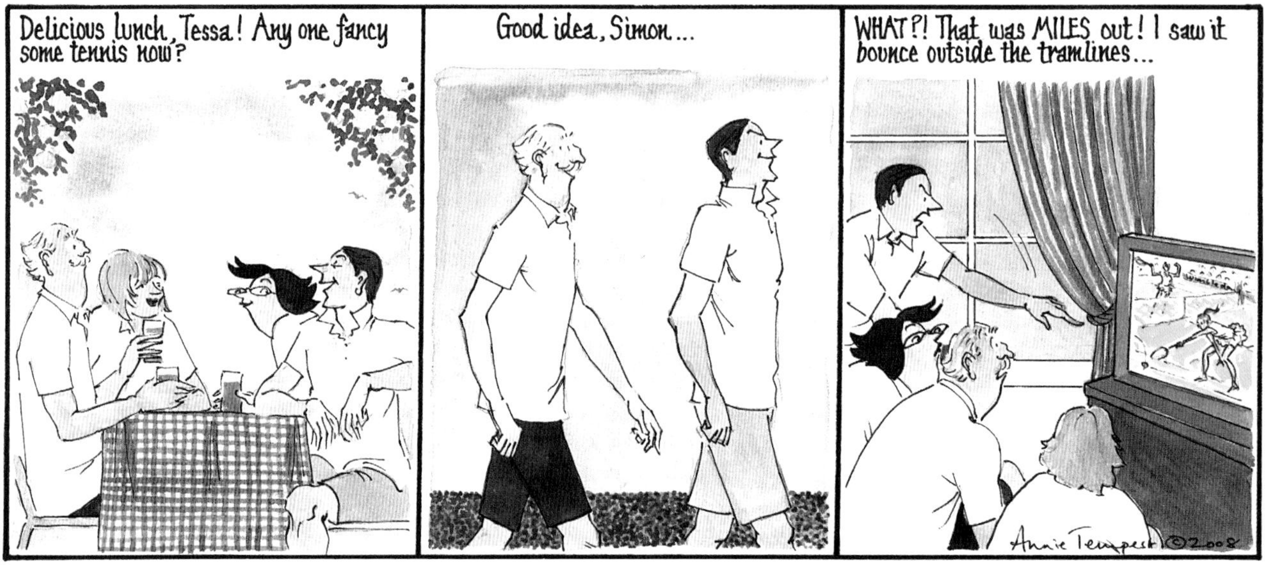
Delicious lunch, Tessa! Any one fancy some tennis now?
Good idea, Simon...
WHAT?! That was MILES out! I saw it bounce outside the tramlines...
Annie Tempest ©2008

JULY

9 Monday

10 Tuesday

11 Wednesday

Last Quarter

Sam ? Garry = Grace
Lunch - 12·45, The Angel, Holmesfield

12 Thursday

Holiday, Northern Ireland
(Battle of the Boyne)

Gen Comm. 7.30pm - The Maynard.

13 Friday

Lunch HERE - JOf!

14 Saturday

Sam/ow P.C. Show - Bakewell

15 Sunday

St Swithin's Day

Bloodhounds Puppy Show.
maggie with Roy in Southampton)

JULY

16 Monday

17 Tuesday

18 Wednesday Barry = Grass

19 Thursday Ladies Luncheon – 1pm

New Moon

20 Friday

First Day of Ramadân

21 Saturday

22 Sunday lunch – Annette – Royal Oak 12:30

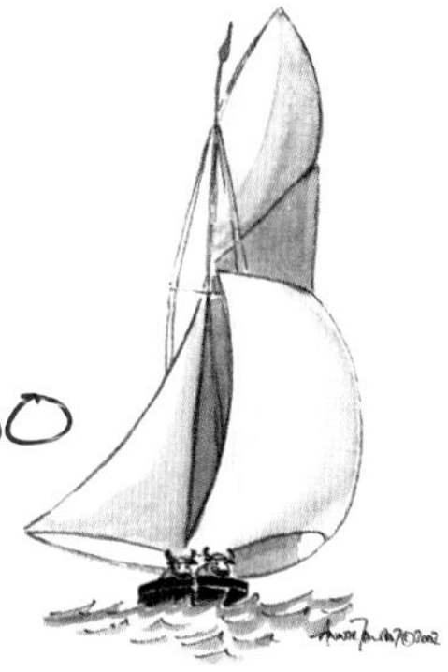

'Cowes...'

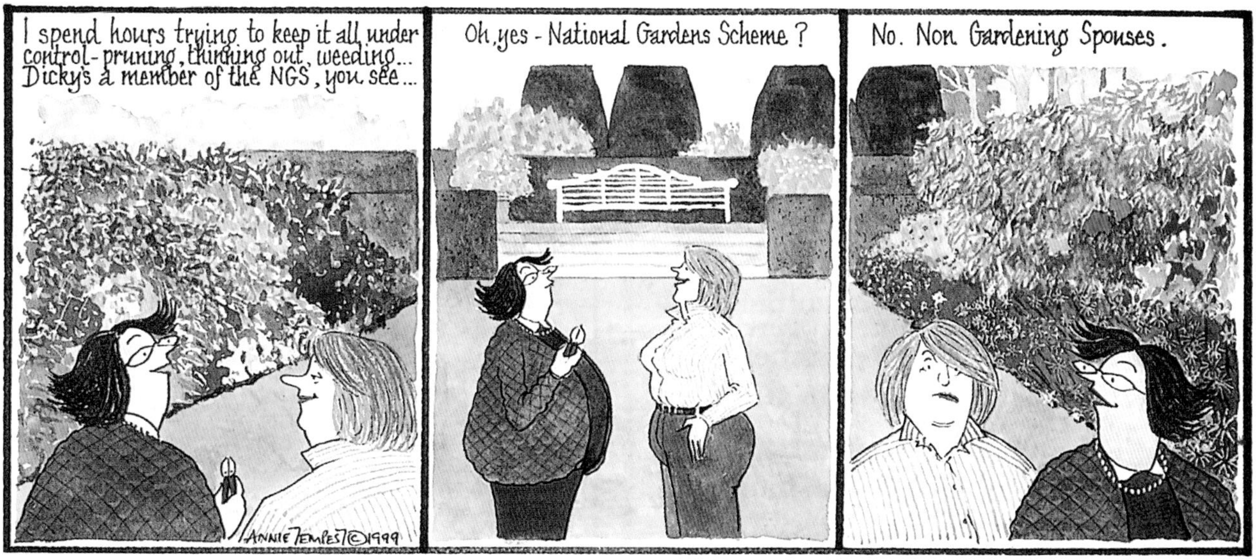
I spend hours trying to keep it all under control - pruning, thinning out, weeding... Dicky's a member of the NGS, you see...
ANNIE TEMPEST © 1999
Oh, yes - National Gardens Scheme ?
No. Non Gardening Spouses.

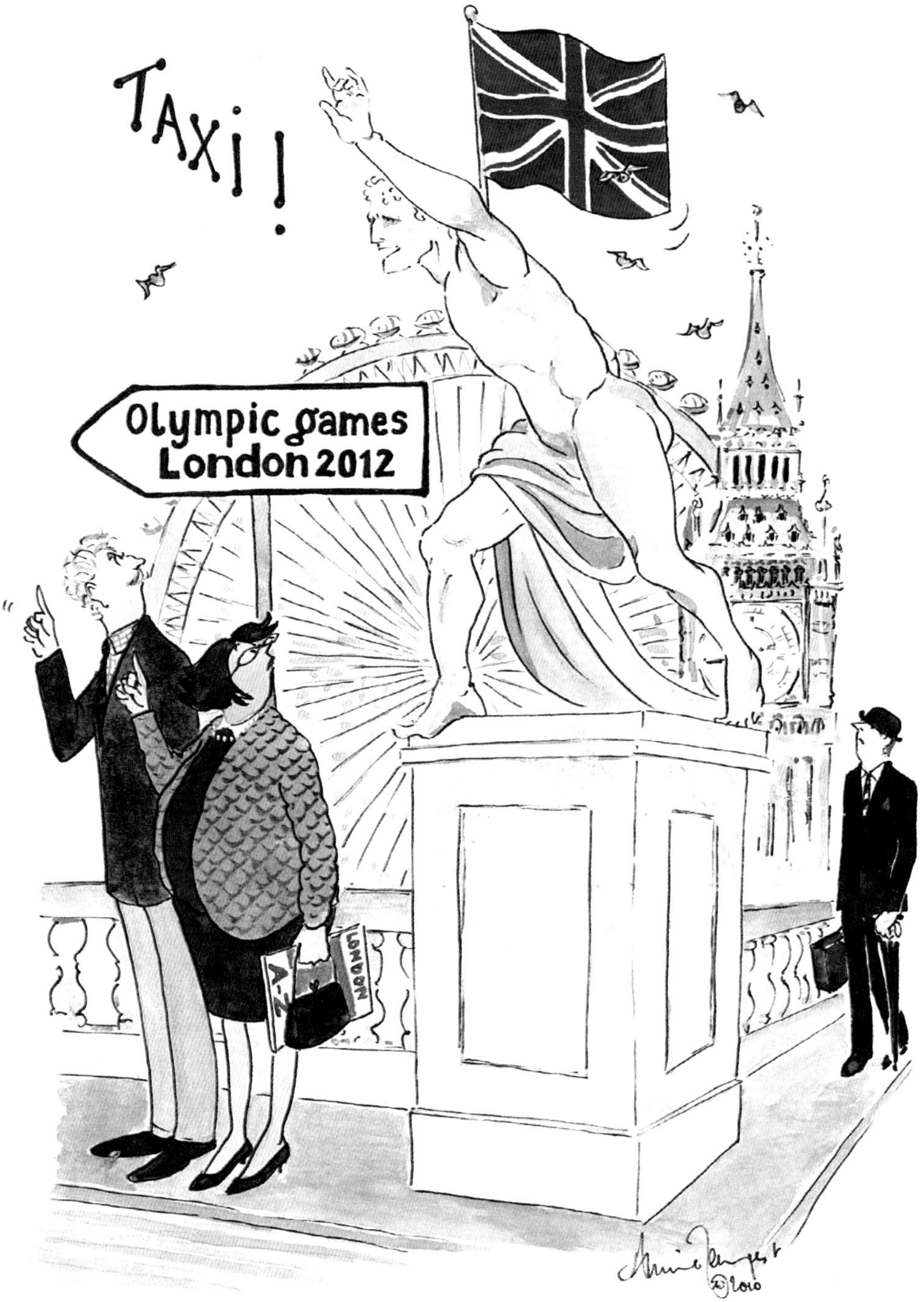
TAXI!
Olympic games
London 2012
A-Z
LONDON

23 Monday

24 Tuesday The Gang - Oxter Bar - 12.30

Sam to R and P

25 Wednesday

Sam to William

26 Thursday *First Quarter*

Sam home

27 Friday JIMMY DIED - 2009 aged 90 *

The Lathkil - 12.30

28 Saturday

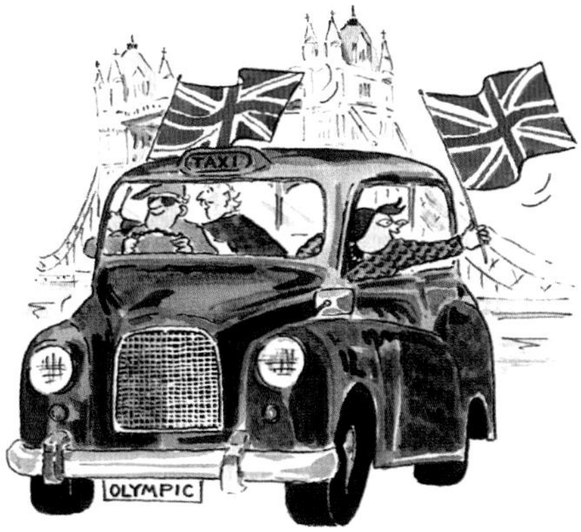
TAXI
OLYMPIC

29 Sunday

JULY - AUGUST

30 Monday

Francis - 4 pm

31 Tuesday

1 Wednesday

2 Thursday ROCK DIED - 2010 - My [illegible] Full Moon

3 Friday

4 Saturday

5 Sunday

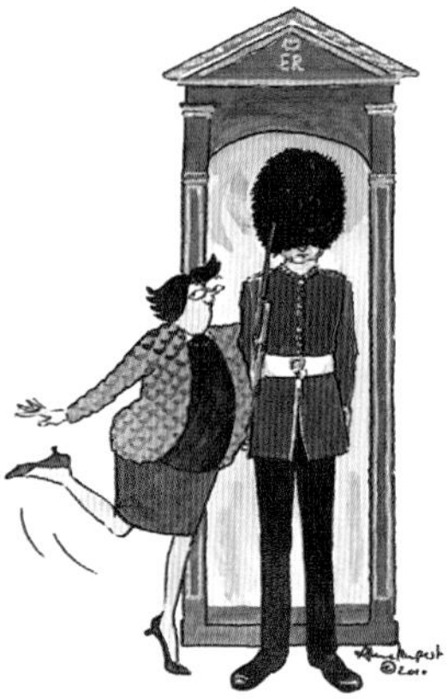

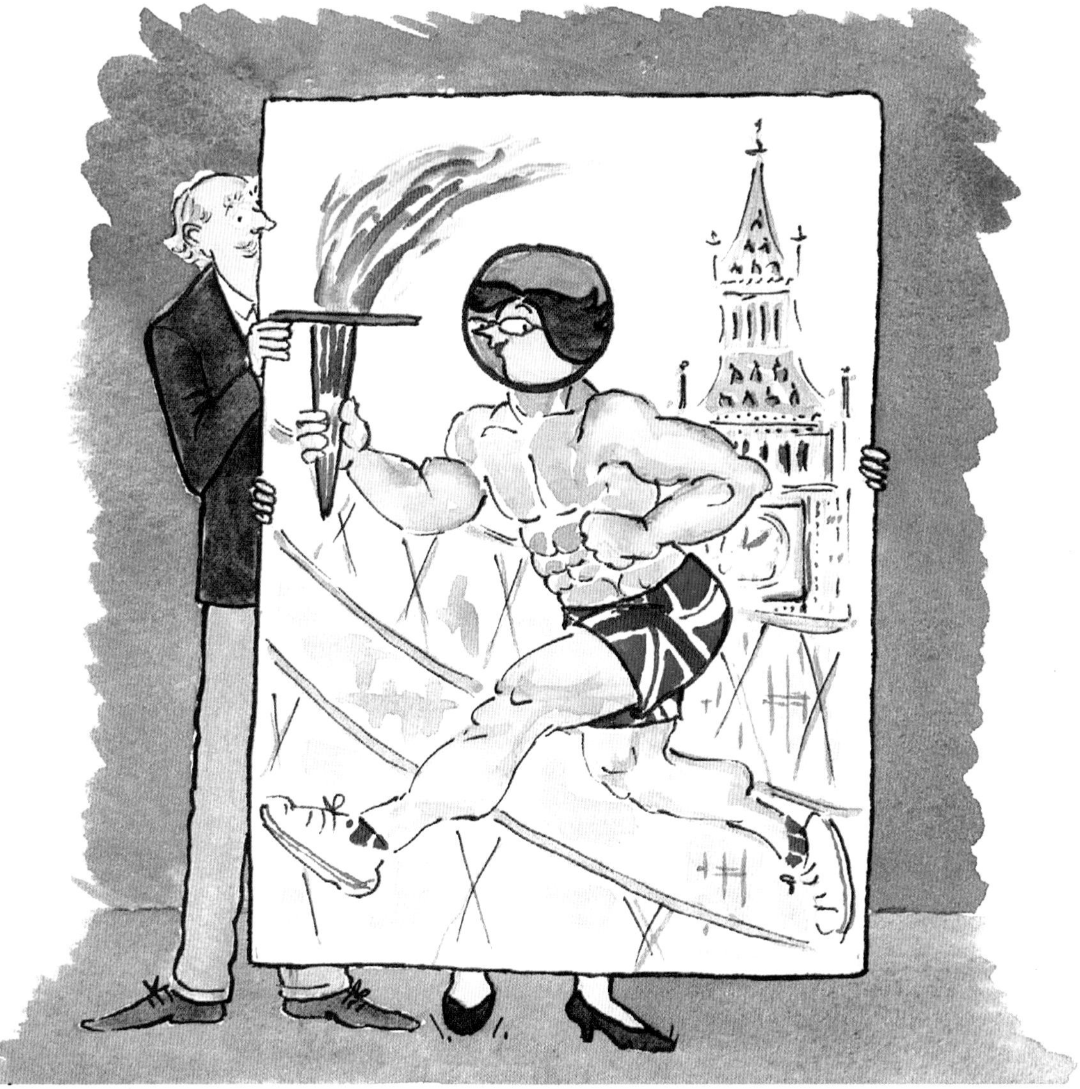

Conversation   Gossip

AUGUST

6 Monday Pick up Car

Summer Bank Holiday, Scotland
Holiday, Republic of Ireland

7 Tuesday last milk delivered.

8 Wednesday

9 Thursday Pat would have been 88 *

Last Quarter

10 Friday The Crispin – no Molly, no Judy

Go to see Car (in old Suburu) 3pm

11 Saturday

12 Sunday

13 Monday
ME - 84 *

The Gang - Peacock - Outer Bar 12.30
meal with Sam, Simon, Celia.

14 Tuesday

15 Wednesday
Sam leaving
2.30 Wed Acton

16 Thursday
lunch with Molly - Ashford - 1 pm

17 Friday
New Moon

Mowcar Head.

Roena and Peter for night.

18 Saturday
Milk recommenced.
Peter and Roena to Settle

19 Sunday
Eid-al-Fitr (end of Ramadãn)

lunch with Annette - Royal Oak

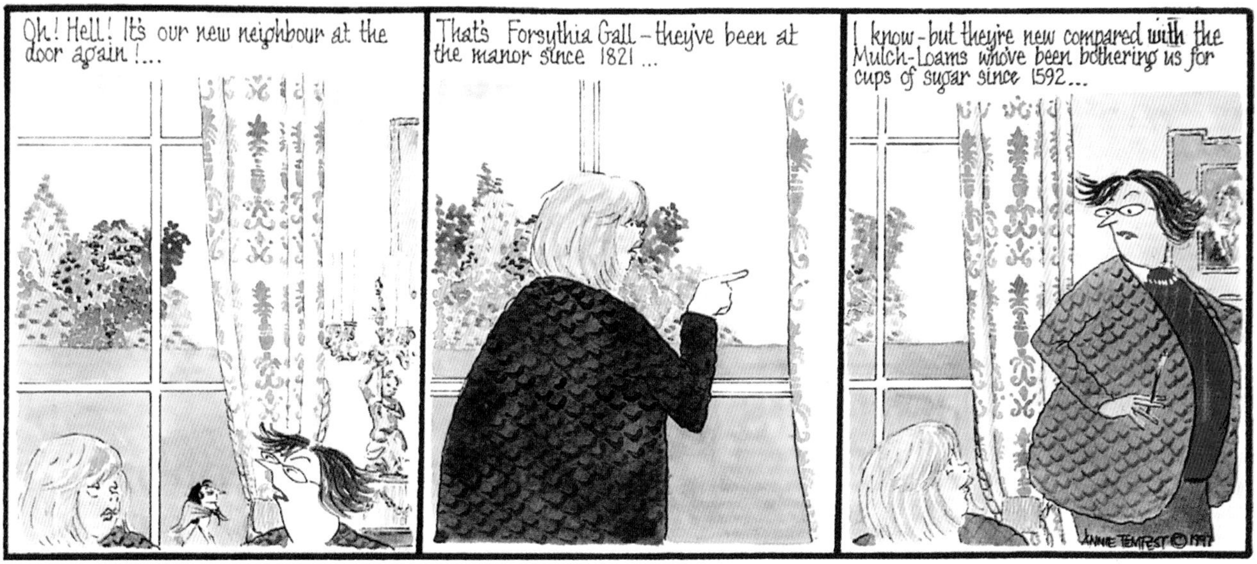
Oh! Hell! It's our new neighbour at the door again!...
That's Forsythia Gall – they've been at the manor since 1821...
I know – but they're new compared with the Mulch-Loams who've been bothering us for cups of sugar since 1592...
ANNIE TEMPEST © 1997

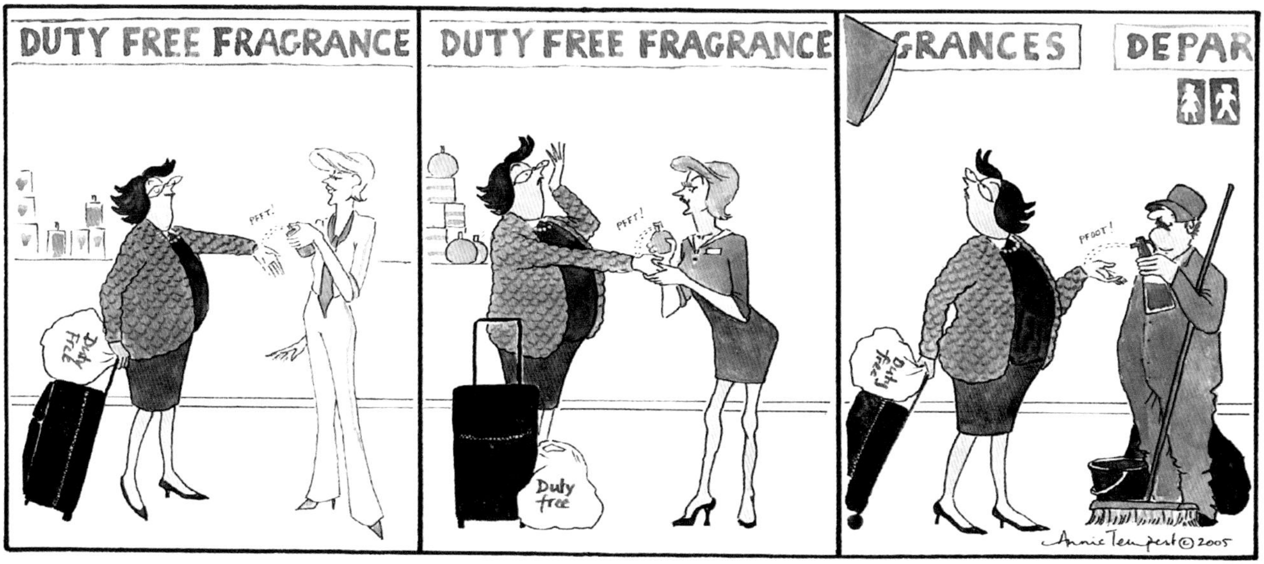
DUTY FREE FRAGRANCE
Duty Free
PFFT.
DUTY FREE FRAGRANCE
PFFT!
Duty free
GRANCES
DEPAR
Duty free
PFOOT!
Annie Tempest © 2005

AUGUST

20 Monday Sam phoned, is in Germany. Lovely day - about 70° Took watch back to Sellors, (Richards) losing time.

21 Tuesday 'Eye place' - 1.30pm

22 Wednesday ANN ANNAT - 93 *

R and P home?

23 Thursday

24 Friday Riverside - Ashford - 12.30

First Quarter

25 Saturday

26 Sunday

Molly and Sue to lunch

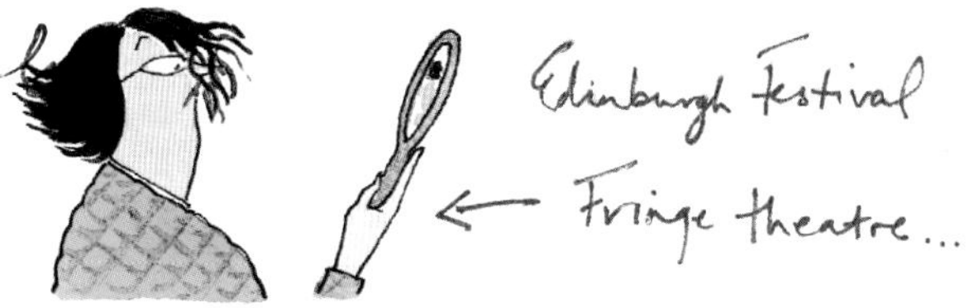
Edinburgh Festival
Fringe theatre...

AUGUST - SEPTEMBER

27 Monday — Summer Bank Holiday, UK (exc. Scotland)

28 Tuesday Diane away

29 Wednesday DOT COURT - 94 * Diane away
To Jo's - lunch - 12:30

30 Thursday

Roena and Peter ?

31 Friday Chatsworth ? — *Full Moon*

1 Saturday R + P

2 Sunday R + P

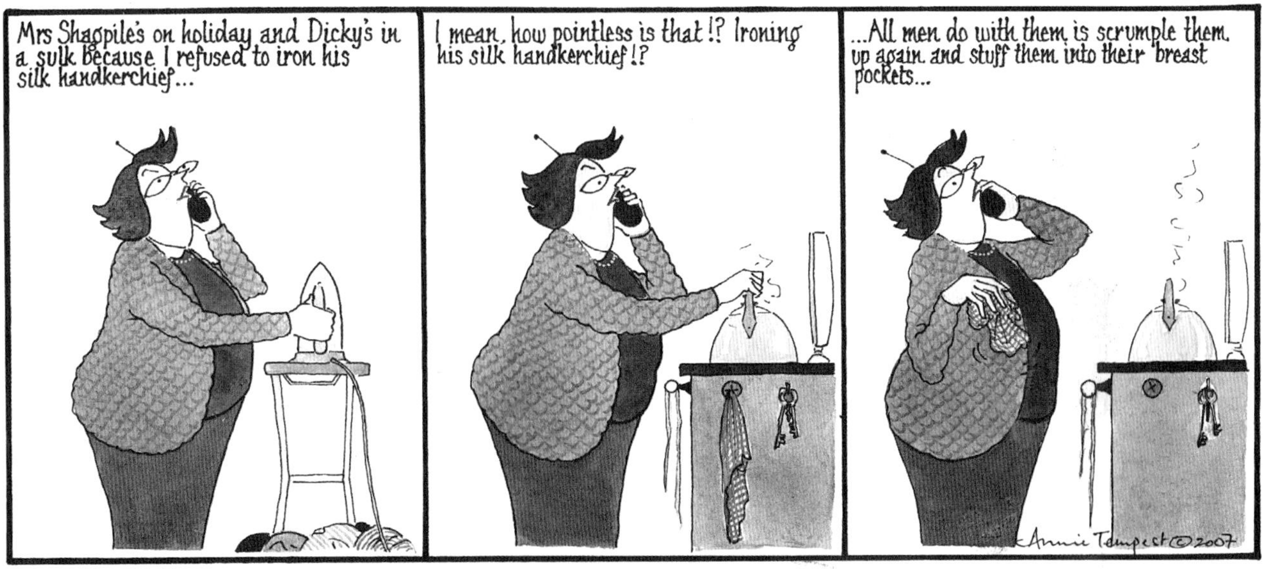
Mrs Shagpile's on holiday and Dicky's in a sulk because I refused to iron his silk handkerchief...
I mean, how pointless is that!? Ironing his silk handkerchief!?
...All men do with them is scrumple them up again and stuff them into their breast pockets...
Annie Tempest © 2007

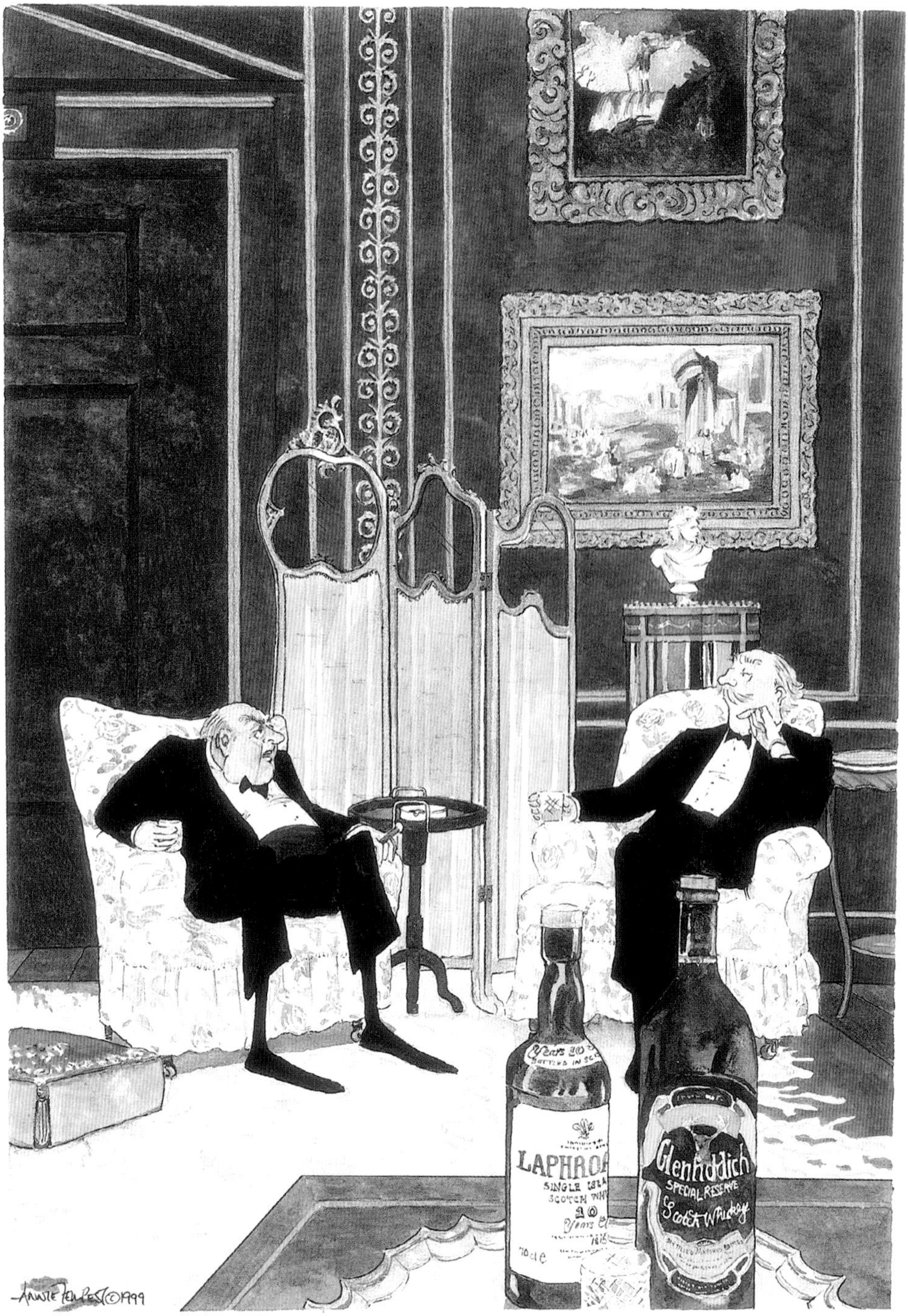
LAPHROAIG
SINGLE ISLAY
SCOTCH WHI
10
Years Old
70cl
Glenfiddich
SPECIAL RESERVE
Scotch Whisky

"... The future's not what it used to be, Dicky..."

SEPTEMBER

3 Monday Wilf: 9 am

Holiday, USA (Labor Day)
Holiday, Canada (Labour Day)

4 Tuesday Giang - The Grouse - 12.30

5 Wednesday MOTHER *

6 Thursday Longshaw

7 Friday Eyre Arms

Ladies Tea - Longshaw

8 Saturday Longshaw

Last Quarter

9 Sunday

SEPTEMBER

10 Monday Diane

11 Tuesday

12 Wednesday Diane

13 Thursday Annette – 88 ✳

14 Friday

15 Saturday

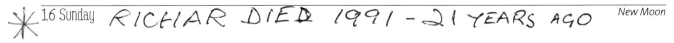

16 Sunday RICHAR DIED 1991 – 21 YEARS AGO *New Moon*

Hartington Wakes – 11am

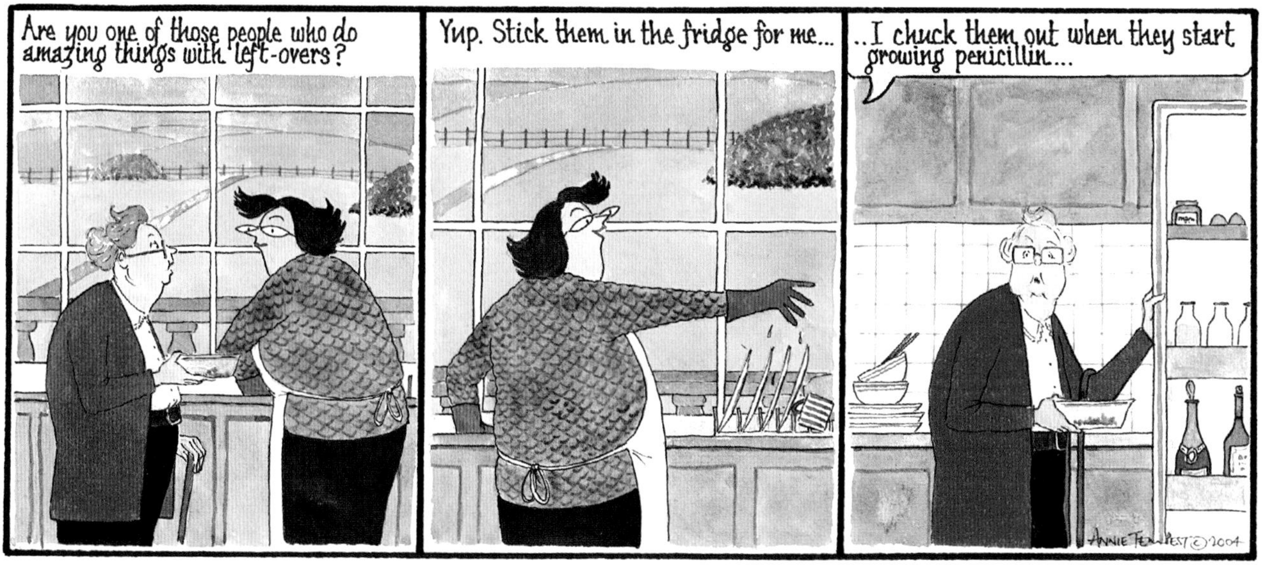
Are you one of those people who do amazing things with left-overs?
Yup. Stick them in the fridge for me...
...I chuck them out when they start growing penicillin...
ANNIE TEMPEST © 2004

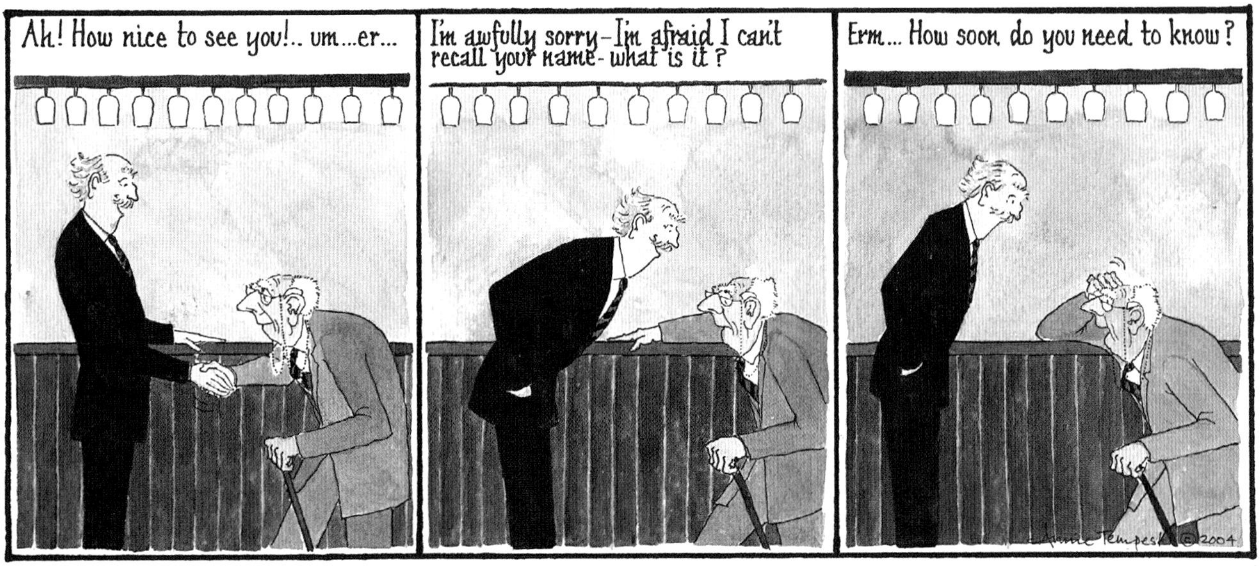
Ah! How nice to see you!.. um...er...
I'm awfully sorry-I'm afraid I can't recall your name- what is it?
Erm... How soon do you need to know?
Annie Tempest © 2004

SEPTEMBER

Diane in ~~Hosp~~.

17 Monday — Jewish New Year (Rosh Hashanah)

18 Tuesday

19 Wednesday

20 Thursday

Ladies luncheon – Mems. ♪ 50s-60s

Gen Comittee – Raymond 8pm

21 Friday ROENA – 57 *

Annette away

22 Saturday ~~Ho~~ The Grouse 9am — *First Quarter* Autumnal Equinox (Autumn begins)

Roena and Peter to Ireland

23 Sunday

24 Monday Ring Trevor

25 Tuesday mach - Trevor ?

26 Wednesday Day of Atonement (Yom Kippur)

27 Thursday

28 Friday

29 Saturday Annette home
The Grouse 8am
Michaelmas Day

Rona and Peter home

30 Sunday Fulwood Booth 9am
Full Moon

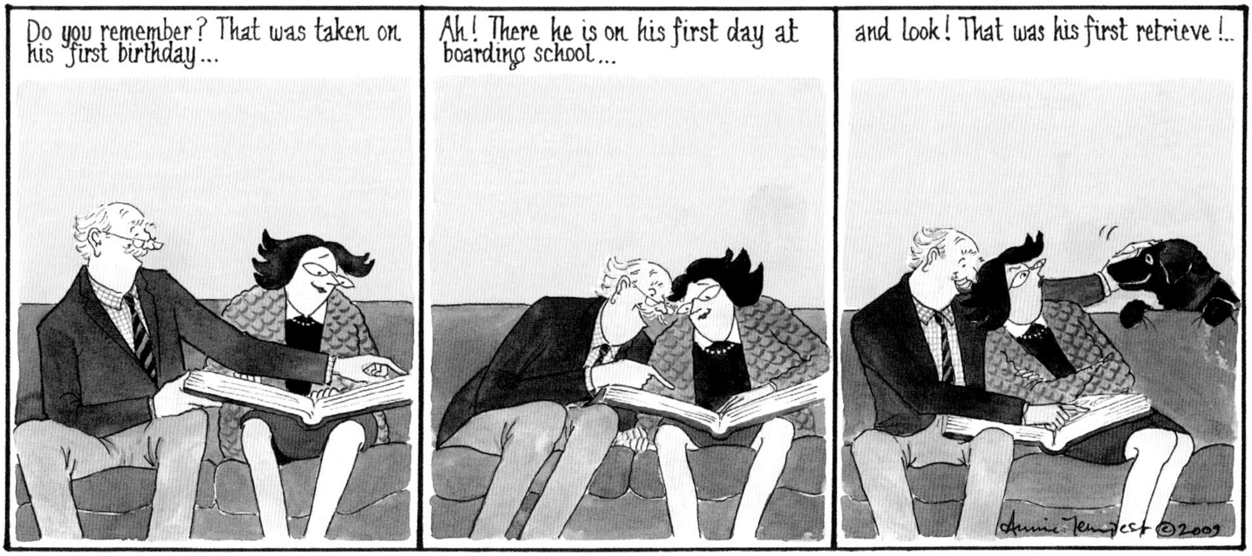
Do you remember? That was taken on his first birthday...
Ah! There he is on his first day at boarding school...
and look! That was his first retrieve!..
Annie Tempest ©2009

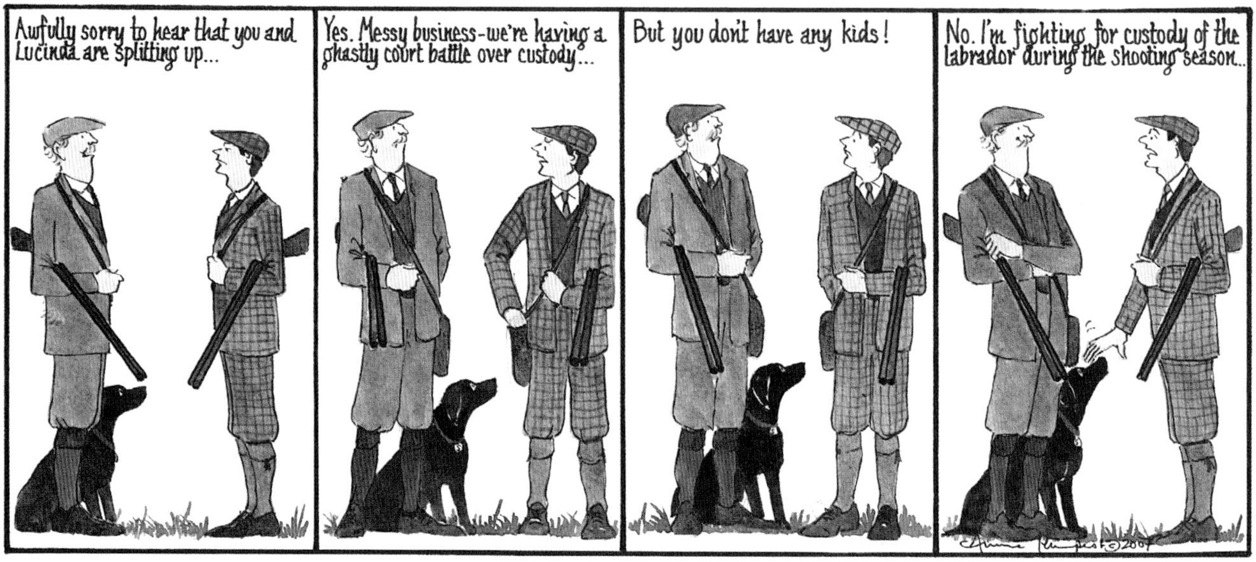
Awfully sorry to hear that you and Lucinda are splitting up...
Yes. Messy business - we're having a ghastly court battle over custody...
But you don't have any kids!
No. I'm fighting for custody of the labrador during the shooting season...

OCTOBER

1 Monday

Holiday, Australia (Labour Day) subject to confirmation
First Day of Tabernacles (Succoth)

2 Tuesday

2.30 - Go for Fair - take recorder

3 Wednesday

4 Thursday

Bolton Cup - Maynard, 8pm.

5 Friday

6 Saturday ? Hayfield

7 Sunday Bamford

OCTOBER

8 Monday

Last Quarter
Holiday, USA (Columbus Day)
Holiday, Canada (Thanksgiving)

9 Tuesday The Bridge - Ford (Ridgeway) The Gang Ranmoor - 10·30 - Shirley Todd's funeral

10 Wednesday

11 Thursday

12 Friday Eyre Arms - 12·30

13 Saturday

14 Sunday Fulwood Booth

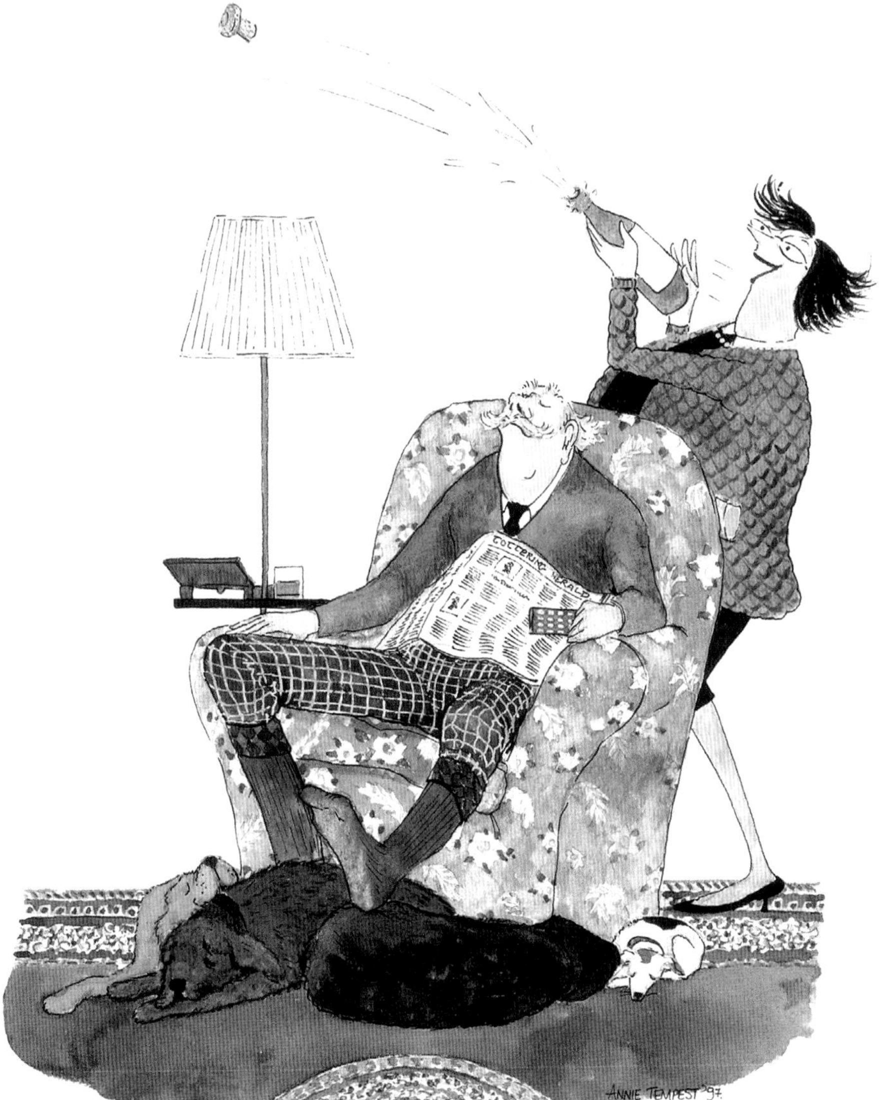
TOTTERING HERALD
ANNIE TEMPEST '97

CORK OVER !...

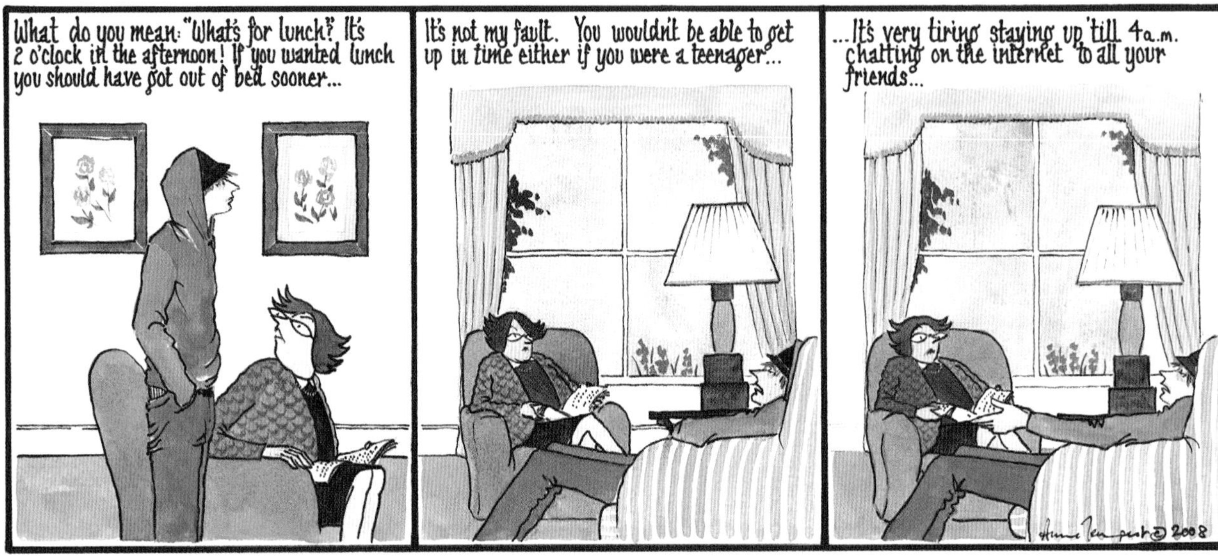
What do you mean: "What's for lunch?" It's 2 o'clock in the afternoon! If you wanted lunch you should have got out of bed sooner...
It's not my fault. You wouldn't be able to get up in time either if you were a teenager...
...It's very tiring staying up 'till 4a.m. chatting on the internet to all your friends...
Anne Tempest © 2008

OCTOBER

15 Monday   *New Moon*

16 Tuesday

17 Wednesday   Ploughing match - where? lunch
Philip Jo.

18 Thursday

19 Friday The Devonshire - Beeley - 12.30

20 Saturday   Peak Forest

21 Sunday

OCTOBER

WEEK 44

22 Monday
First Quarter
Holiday, New Zealand (Labour Day)

23 Tuesday Molly - Hassop

24 Wednesday No Nigel - Boiler, etc.
United Nations Day

25 Thursday

26 Friday Rowleys - 12.30

27 Saturday Dovedale

28 Sunday Kennels - Sumnil Moor
British Summer Time ends

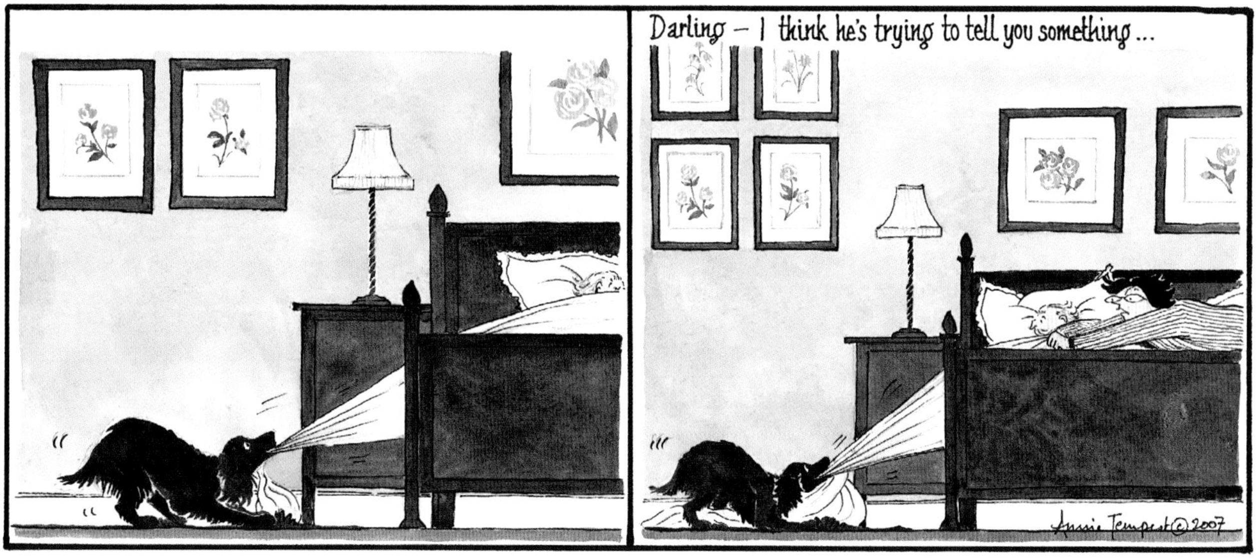
Darling – I think he's trying to tell you something ...
Annie Tempest © 2007

Where on earth did I put my jelly bag?..
JELLYS & JAMS
Trick or Treat?..
Annie Tempest © 2009

29 Monday
Full Moon
Holiday, Republic of Ireland

FATHER *

The Peacock - Barton 12.30-1, Boffins.

30 Tuesday
The Bridge - Ford - 12.30 - The Gang.

31 Wednesday
Hallowe'en

1 Thursday
All Saints' Day

2 Friday
Eyre Arms - Halsop - 12.30

3 Saturday BARBARA (DONCASTE) - 59 *
Hayfield

4 Sunday
Bamford
4 Shires Opening   Meet_ Hulland Ward -
                        Paul Harrison

NOVEMBER

5 Monday — Guy Fawkes

4pm Dominic Stanniforth - here - files etc.

6 Tuesday Barlow Opening Meet

7 Wednesday — *Last Quarter*

8 Thursday

9 Friday MOLLY - 85 *
The Devonshire Arms - Pilsley

10 Saturday Fullwood Booth

11 Sunday Annette away — Remembrance Sunday
~~Ed~~ Longshaw - Belton Cup.

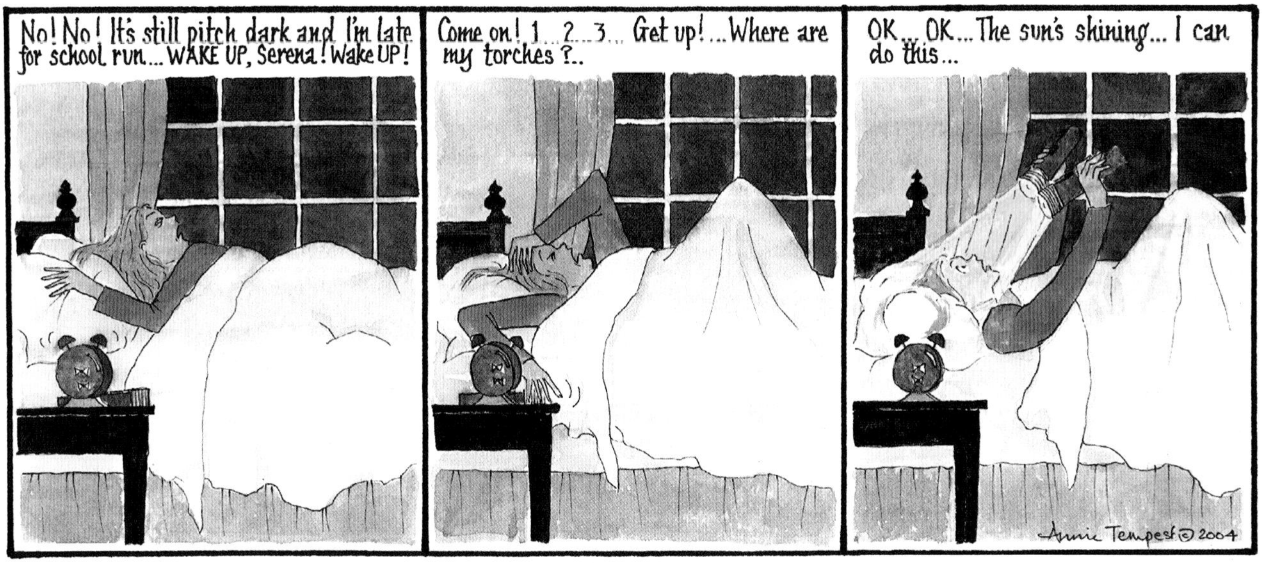
No! No! It's still pitch dark and I'm late for school run... WAKE UP, Serena! Wake UP!
Come on! 1... 2... 3... Get up!... Where are my torches?..
OK... OK... The sun's shining... I can do this...
Annie Tempest © 2004

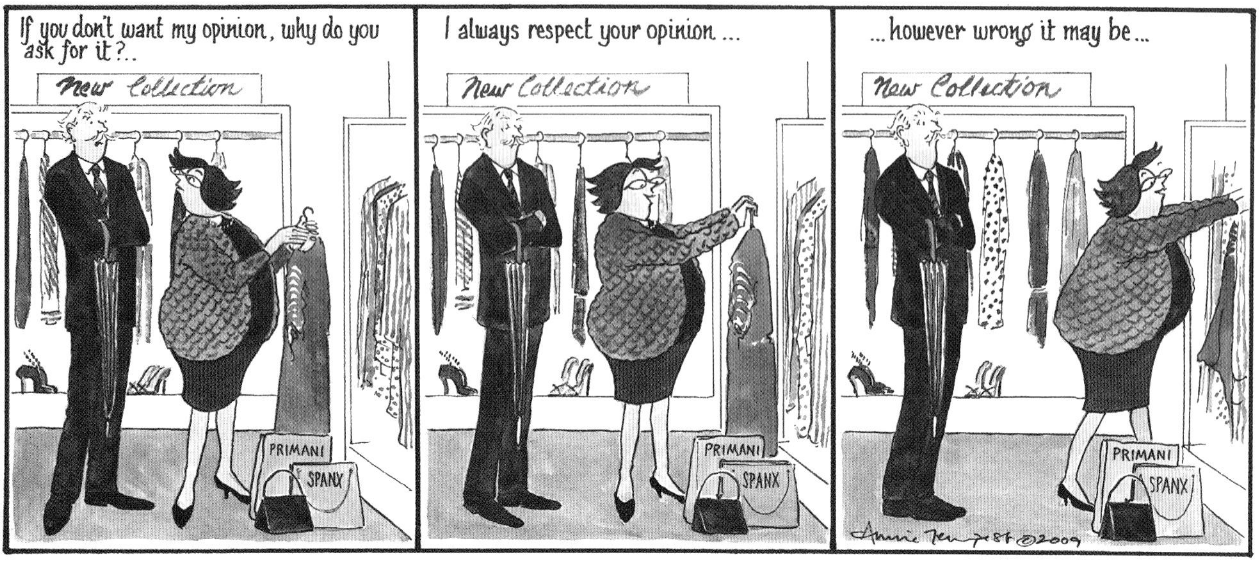
If you don't want my opinion, why do you ask for it?..
New Collection
PRIMANI
SPANX
I always respect your opinion ...
New Collection
PRIMANI
SPANX
... however wrong it may be ...
New Collection
PRIMANI
SPANX
©2009

NOVEMBER

12 Monday — Holiday, USA (Veterans Day) / Holiday, Canada (Remembrance Day)

13 Tuesday — Kate to Vet - 2.30 — *New Moon*

14 Wednesday

15 Thursday — Islamic New Year begins (subject to sighting of the moon)

Ladies luncheon - Mary Queen of Scots - 12.30 - 1pm
Rutland.

16 Friday

Roena ?

17 Saturday — Dovedale

Roena

18 Sunday — DICK HORNE - 86 *

Roena

19 Monday Phyll Joel - would have been 98 *
Diane

Roena

20 Tuesday - The Gang - The Rising Sun, Abbey Lane, 12:30

Roena going home

First Quarter

21 Wednesday
No Diane

2 pm - Hairdresser

22 Thursday 11·40 Dentist

Holiday, USA (Thanksgiving Day)

23 Friday

24 Saturday Hounds - Pearsons
Peak Forest

25 Sunday Hounds - Crich

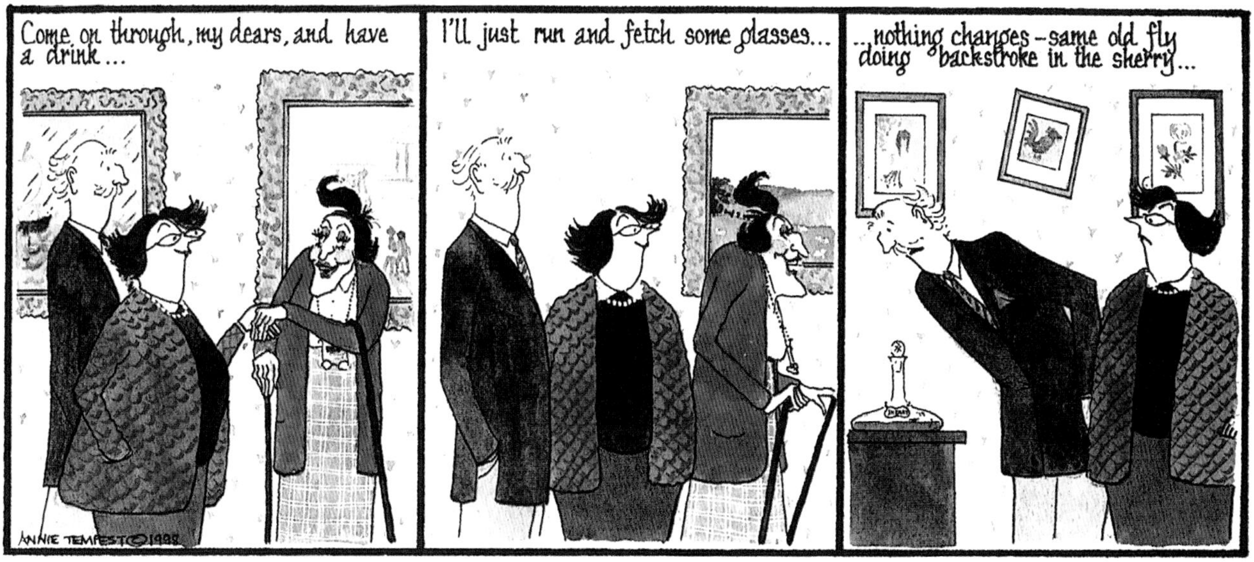
Come on through, my dears, and have a drink...
ANNIE TEMPEST © 1998
I'll just run and fetch some glasses...
...nothing changes – same old fly doing backstroke in the sherry...

You go ahead - I'm waiting for Trenchfoot - we're lunching together...

Ah! Tottering! Decided not to wait for Willie, eh!

Just remembered I went to his memorial two weeks ago...

26 Monday

27 Tuesday

28 Wednesday Dentist - 11.30 *Full Moon*

29 Thursday

30 Friday The Rutland *St Andrew's Day*

1 Saturday Old people' lunch
Dovedale - Championship.

2 Sunday CELIA - 43 ✳ Nick Swift. *First Sunday in Advent*

DECEMBER

---

3 Monday

5pm. Claremont, Mr. Getty.

---

4 Tuesday

Farmers Garage - 2pm - Oil, Suburu.

---

5 Wednesday Annette home.

---

6 Thursday *Last Quarter*

---

7 Friday

---

8 Saturday

---

9 Sunday Nick Dennifs *Hannukah begins*

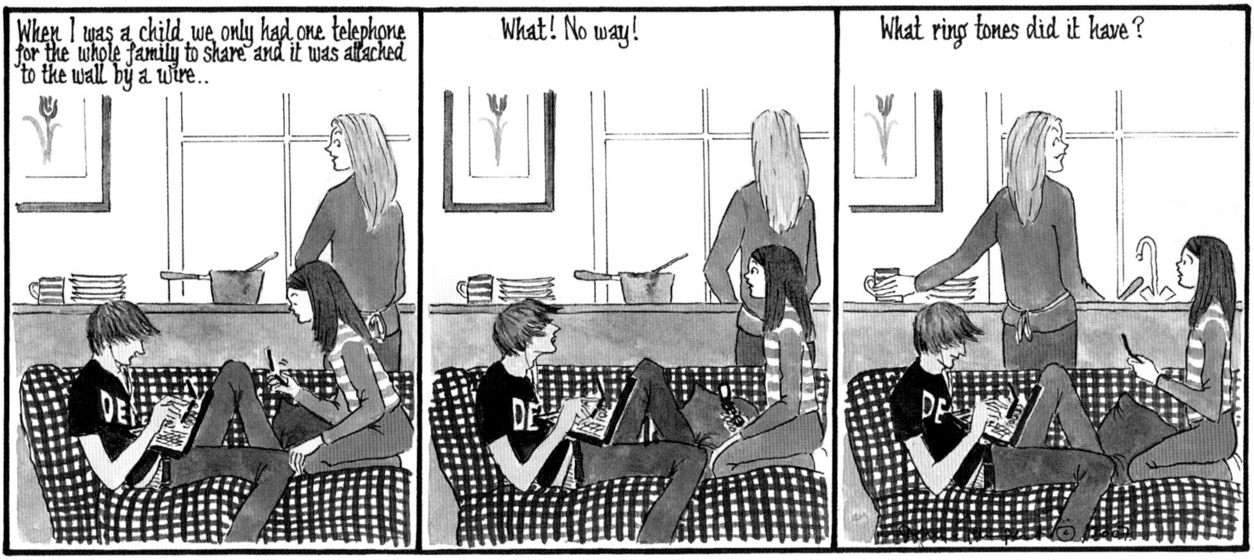
When I was a child we only had one telephone for the whole family to share and it was attached to the wall by a wire..
What! No way!
What ring tones did it have?

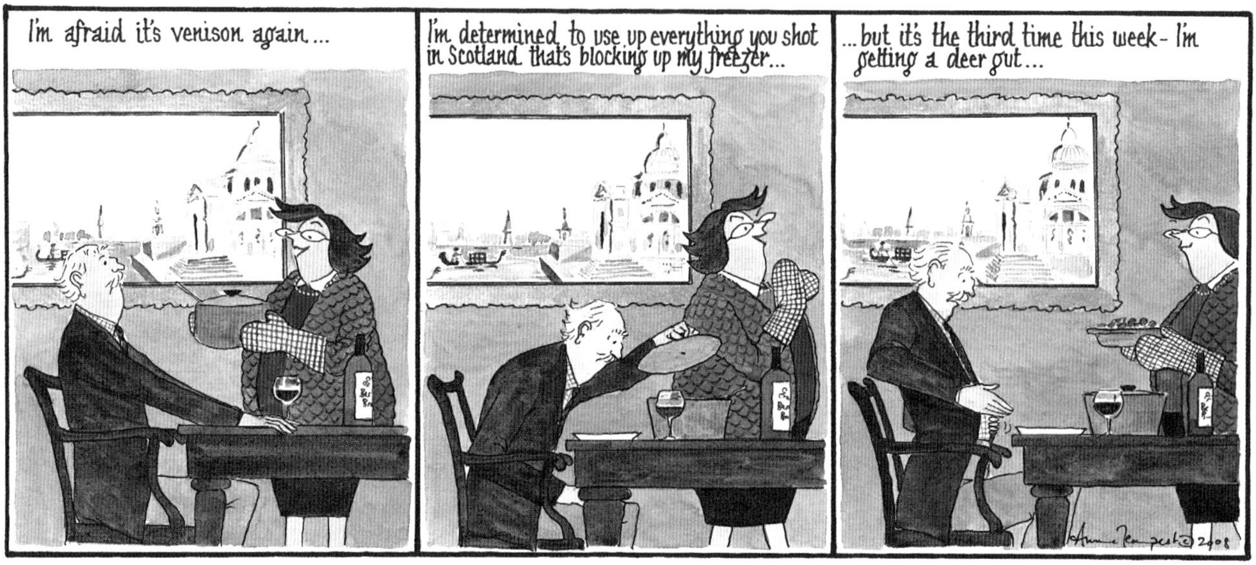
I'm afraid it's venison again...
I'm determined to use up everything you shot in Scotland that's blocking up my freezer...
...but it's the third time this week- I'm getting a deer gut...

DECEMBER

---

10 Monday

---

11 Tuesday The Gang - Norfolk Arms - 12.30

---

12 Wednesday

---

13 Thursday ~~Judy - 8~~ *New Moon*

Ladies luncheon (2 Gifts)

---

14 Friday Judy - 86 ✳ The Rutland

---

15 Saturday SIMON - 53 ✳

---

16 Sunday Nick Deniff.

DECEMBER

17 Monday The Peacock · Barlow - 12-30 Boffins.
for 1pm

18 Tuesday

19 Wednesday

20 Thursday Sam - ish ?

First Quarter

21 Friday

Winter Solstice (Winter begins)

22 Saturday

Francis - 5pm ish

23 Sunday Hounds - Organ Ground
Sue Hilyards - lunch time - 12:30

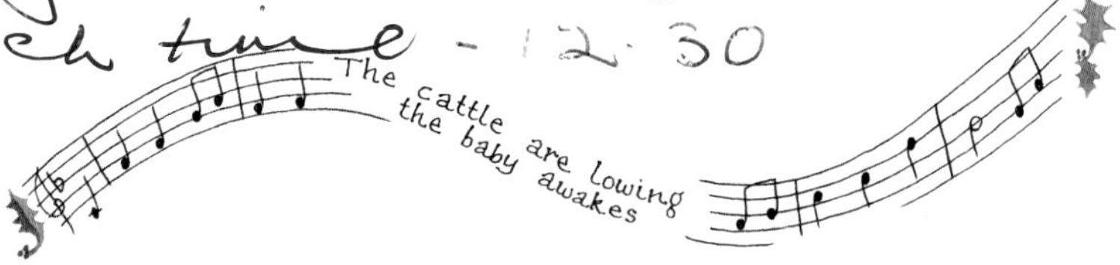
The cattle are lowing
the baby awakes

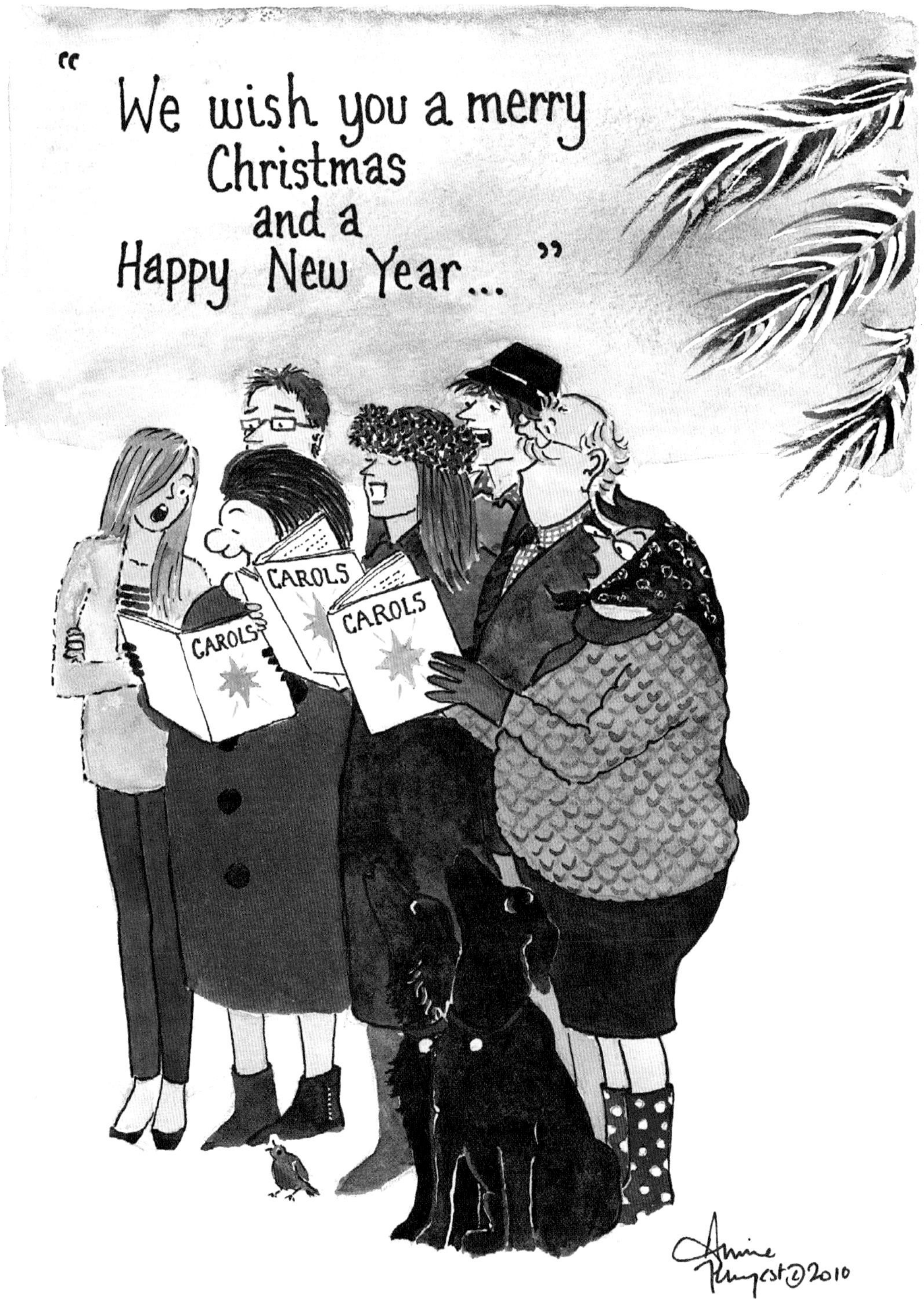

" We wish you a merry Christmas and a Happy New Year... "
CAROLS
CAROLS
CAROLS
Annie Tempest © 2010

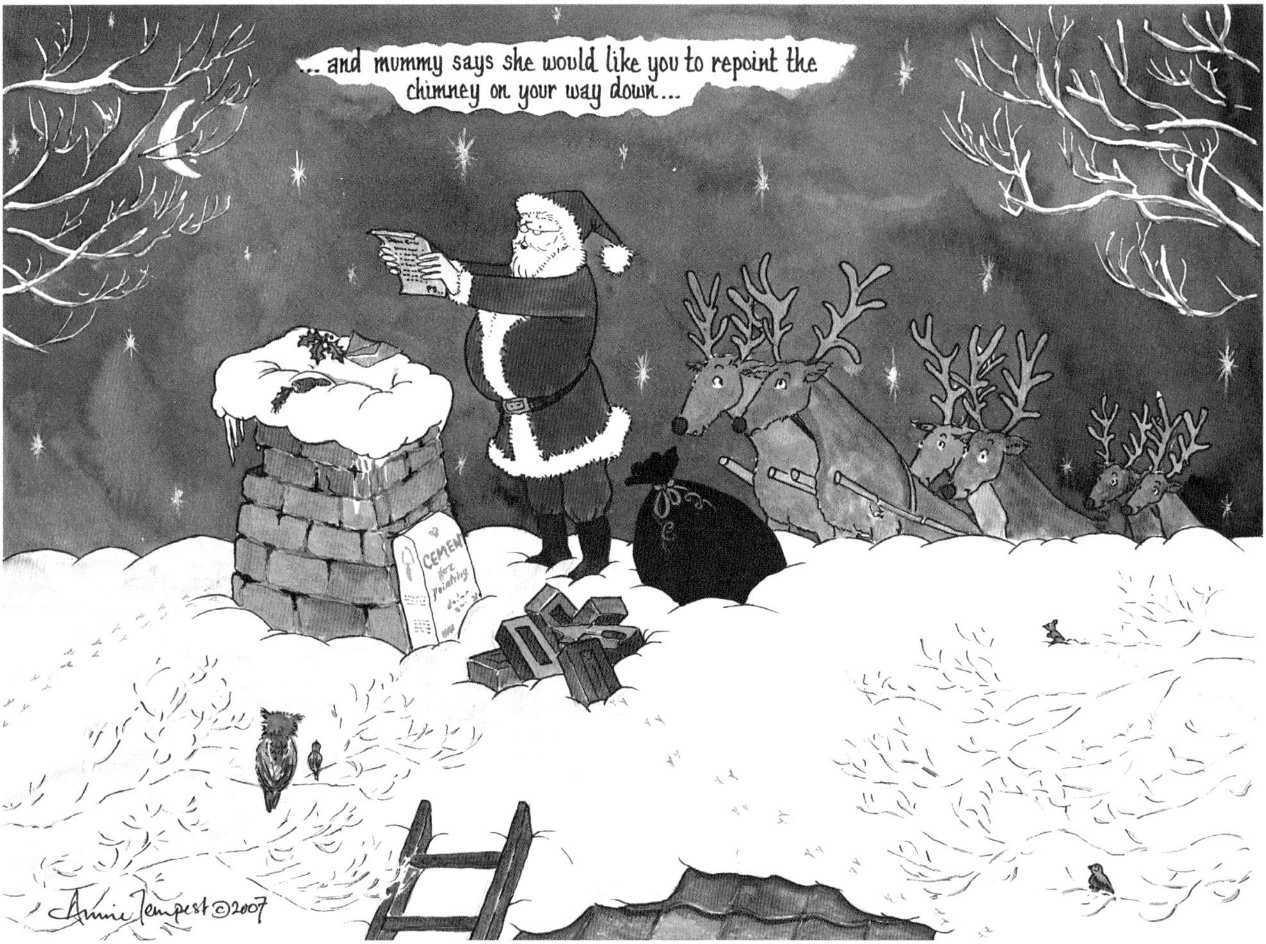
... and mummy says she would like you to repoint the chimney on your way down...
Annie Tempest ©2007

DECEMBER

24 Monday   Christmas Eve

25 Tuesday   Christmas Day
Holiday, UK, Republic of Ireland, USA, Canada,
Australia and New Zealand

26 Wednesday Hounds - Ashbourne Bicester   Boxing Day (St Stephen's Day)
cancelled   Holiday, UK, Republic of Ireland,
Australia and New Zealand

27 Thursday

28 Friday   *Full Moon*

29 Saturday

30 Sunday

DECEMBER – JANUARY

31 Monday — New Year's Eve

1 Tuesday — Flagg – Hounds – Barton — New Year's Day
Crate Inn — Holiday, UK, Republic of Ireland, USA, Canada, Australia and New Zealand

2 Wednesday — Diane — Holiday, Scotland and New Zealand

3 Thursday — Diane

4 Friday

5 Saturday — *Last Quarter*

6 Sunday — Hounds – Thornbridge — Epiphany